THE HOLY POTHOLES OF CHRISTIANITY

To: Ron + Lana

Enjoy your Spiritual Journey

Albert Schuessler

Eph. 3:16

God Bless!

THE HOLY POTHOLES OF CHRISTIANITY

Does Christianity Work, or Will It Trip You Up?

Albert Schuessler

Unless otherwise indicated, Scripture quotations used in this book are taken from the King James Version of the Bible (public domain).

Scripture quotations marked "NIV" are taken from the Holy Bible, New International Version®. Copyright © 1973, 1978, 1984, 2011 by Biblica, Inc.™ Used by permission of Zondervan. All rights reserved worldwide.

Scripture quotations marked "NASB" are taken from the New American Standard Bible®, © The Lockman Foundation 1960, 1962, 1963, 1968, 1971, 1972, 1973, 1975, 1977, 1995. Used by permission.

Scripture quotations marked "NLT" are taken from the Holy Bible, New Living Translation, copyright © 1996, 2004, 2007. Used by permission of Tyndale House Publishers, Inc. Carol Stream, Illinois 60188. All rights reserved.

Scripture quotations marked "NKJV" are taken from The New King James Version. © 1982 by Thomas Nelson, Inc. Used by permission. All rights reserved.

Scripture quotations marked "GW" are taken from God's Word®, © 1995 God's Word to the Nations. Used by permission of Baker Publishing Group. All rights reserved.

Scripture quotations marked "ESV" are taken from The English Standard Version. © 2001 by Crossway Bibles, a division of Good News Publishers. Used by permission. All rights reserved.

Copyright © 2014 Albert Schuessler
All rights reserved.

ISBN: 0692248641
ISBN 13: 978-0692248645
Library of Congress Control Number: 2014912385
Heartburn Cafe, Valley Center, KS

This book is dedicated to my wife of fifty-six years, Shirley Schuessler.

Outside of the Holy Spirit, you have been the GPS of my life, guiding me through the potholes of Christianity. Thanks for your wisdom and strength in my life. Many times I took the wrong turn in life, and you recalculated my directions and got me back on the road again.

With love and respect to you!

Contents

Preface ix
Acknowledgments xi
Introduction xiii

Part 1: Know the Culprit
Damaging Potholes

Chapter 1: A Collision 3
Chapter 2: A Clash 13
Chapter 3: A Culprit 23
Chapter 4: A Clue 31

Part 2: Learn to Navigate
Driving through the Potholes

Chapter 5: A Corrupt Heart 47
Chapter 6: A Confused Heart 63
Chapter 7: A Curious Heart 73
Chapter 8: A Consuming Heart 83

Part 3: Live the Victory
Defying the Potholes

Chapter 9: A Changed Heart 95
Chapter 10: A Clean Heart 105
Chapter 11: A Contrite Heart 117

About the Author 131

Preface

After having the privilege of spending forty-five years in full-time Christian service and pastoring two churches in Kansas and one in the Washington, DC, area, I realized I had touched many lives. Ministering to individuals as well as complete families is rewarding. I am with them when they receive Christ as their Savior, when they are baptized, when they get married, when they have children in the hospital — and yes, when they pass away.

After retiring from full-time ministry, I realized I missed having personal contact with people. It seemed like a waste of time not to use the vast reservoir of spiritual life I had experienced. At that time God challenged me to share that information with people in written form. Seven years ago I accepted the challenge, and this book had its beginning. It seemed like a long journey, but it was well worth the time and effort.

People of all ages and walks of life are my desired target for this book. This book will challenge Christian leaders as well as those who walk through the doors of a church Sunday after Sunday. To individuals or their family members who've been hurt by the potholes of Christianity, my prayer is that you will read this book and begin the process of healing in your life.

My challenge is that you will begin this incredible journey called Christianity.

Acknowledgments

To My Parents

Thanks to my mom and dad. Thank you for living your lives in a way that pointed me to Christ, not only by what you said, but more importantly by what you did. You gave me a great brother and three fabulous sisters. You are my heroes.

I always wanted to be just like you!

To My Family

Thanks to my three sons and their wives, my grandchildren, and my great-grandchildren. Thank you for the love and support you've given me during my forty-six years in ministry. Despite the times I neglected you as a father and pastor, you never complained.

I have a tremendous love for each one of you!

To My Pastor and His Family

Thanks to Pastor Bruce Thomas and his wife, Lesley. You have helped me transition from the pulpit to the pew gracefully. Thanks for giving me the opportunity to continue in ministry during retirement and for allowing me to go from the pew to the pulpit occasionally. I have great respect for you and consider you my friend.

The eighteenth green decides the winner.

To My Sister

Thanks to my sister, Joyce Schuessler Yock. Thank you for your help in providing technological expertise and financial assistance to help me achieve my dream. You will reap the benefits.

I appreciate the support you have given me on this project.

To My Proofreaders

Thanks to Nancy Landes and Ashley Krier, who dedicated many hours to proofreading and editing this book before sending the manuscript to the publishing company.

Thank you for being patient with me.

Introduction

This book is about traveling down the road of Christianity without becoming a victim of an accident and ultimately becoming another statistic — someone who ended up on the side of the road, broken down, and unable to move forward in his or her Christian journey. The journey can be overwhelming and cause life failures that will shut down our Christian lives if we lack understanding. It can cause overheated engines, burned-out wheel bearings, run-down batteries, flat tires, vapor lock, broken universal joints, and many other stresses and failures that cause us to pull off to the side of the road and shut down.

During summers while growing up on a farm in south-central Kansas, I experienced the yearly thrill of driving down the dusty dirt road and encountering the danger of a washboard road filled with potholes. I remember how it jarred my teeth and shook the steering wheel; at times the road even jerked the steering wheel out of my hand, causing me to end up in the ditch. I remember going fast and experiencing the thrill of going airborne. However, I sometimes ended up on the side of the road with a damaged vehicle, unable to continue my trip.

In this book I take this experience and parallel it to the experiences I've had of traveling down the dusty, washboard, pothole-filled road of Christianity. In my Christian journey, I've had the airborne experience and the thrill of an abundant life, in which I soared high in my relationship with Christ. However, I also recall times when the road got bumpy, the washboard was rough, and the potholes were deep — in fact so deep that I lost control of the wheel, pulled over to the side of the road, and turned Christianity off. Maybe that was the problem — I lost control of the wheel.

While sitting alongside the road in my journey, I had come to the place where I asked the question, "Does Christianity work?" I had become a casualty of the potholes and the washboard. There may be those reading this book who have asked the same question at some point in their Christian journey. Now that many years have passed, I can honestly say I've learned a few driving principles regarding how to avoid the potholes of Christian life; I share those in the chapters of this book.

I have found that the difference between the thrill and agony of Christianity is only eighteen inches. Yes, that's the eighteen inches from the head to the heart. It's not a long or difficult journey, but it's a necessary one. It's a journey of change, transformation, and transparency that will allow you to go airborne and soar in your journey in a way you've never soared before. I've come to the conclusion that yes, Christianity actually *does* work.

Let the journey begin. Enjoy the read.

Part 1
Know the Culprit

Damaging Potholes

When we first become Christians, I don't think the thought ever enters our minds that there might be danger lying ahead in our Christian journey. To imagine a culprit lurking in the path of our journey would seem sacrilegious. Don't Christian leaders often put forth the message that once you become a Christian, everything will be great?

If you look back into the annals of Christianity from its conception, you will find many casualties in the Bible as well as in history books. Some people either were unaware of the potholes or decided they would ignore them. Though many tripped and stumbled in the potholes, I'm glad God's grace could lift them up, dust them off, and send them on their journey once again.

People who have knowledge are able to make the right decisions. In the next few chapters, I expose the "culprit" and the damage he is able to cause. So that we may know the culprit, reading these chapters closely is important.

Chapter 1

A Collision

*A Collision at the Corner of Christianity and Life
Does Christianity Work?*

I find then a law, that evil is present with me, the one who wills to do good. For I delight in the law of God according to the inward man. But I see another law in my members, warring against the law of my mind, and bringing me into captivity to the law of sin which is in my members. O wretched man that I am! Who will deliver me from this body of death?
—Rom. 7:21–24 NKJV

Therefore do not cast away your confidence, which has great reward. For you have need of endurance, so that after you have done the will of God, you may receive the promise.
—Heb. 10:35–36 NKJV

The Question

Does Christianity work? That is the question I've struggled with for a number of years in my life. That question was triggered in my mind one day as I was traveling down the highway of my Christian journey and had a collision at the corner of Christianity and my life. It was more than a fender bender; my life was headed for the junkyard. That collision left me with a question I had to have answered if I were going to continue down the road of spiritual life and growth.

I was stymied in my spiritual growth and found myself floundering, trying to move forward but unable to advance even one spiritual inch. Because of this experience, I set out to find a way to move forward and get out of this spiritual quagmire. God was very gracious to provide me with the answer to this question, even though it came by way of a very painful period of my life. I share the painful experience God used to answer this ever-nagging question I had about Christianity to help others who may struggle with this same question in their lives today: "Does Christianity work?"

How Heart-Aching Can the Question Be?

In my personal experiences, I've discovered and believe it to be true that the Christian life should be lived and experienced from the heart, which the Bible considers the inner being or spiritual part of a person, and not from the head, which the Bible considers the physical brain or the intellectual part of a person. If we're extremely stubborn and decide to bypass living from the heart because we're so determined to live life from the head, we can be assured that we most certainly will experience the heartache Paul spoke of in Romans 7:21–24. He described in his own words and demonstrated in his own life just how wretched life can be.

More important than my personal experiences is the fact that God makes it very clear in His word that life should be lived from the heart. "Keep thy heart with all diligence; for out of it are the issues of life" (Prov. 4:23). The writer makes it clear that life issues flow from the heart rather than from the head. Someone once said to me, "He didn't need more knowledge of the Bible. What he needed was to have an understanding of how to apply that knowledge to his life."

A Collision

It's easy, especially living in today's self-centered culture, to get the biblical style of relating and living reversed. There's a tendency to try our best to live the Christian life from the head rather than from the heart. In the process we develop a superficial system for our relationships. In other words our relationships aren't deep; therefore we interact with one another and with God through only a head-to-head-based relationship.

When we interact with each other using this confrontational head-to-head approach in every area of our relationships, we find that this approach may work for a while, but the system will eventually break down. When this happens we realize that the Christian life we always dreamed of attaining isn't working out like we thought it would or should. At this point we can become disillusioned with Christianity and also very angry. We can either continue in our anger for a long period of time or become so angry that we simply walk away from God for a season. When this happens we're then apt to lose confidence in ourselves and may even have moments when we lose our confidence in God to enable us to live our lives with purpose. It's then very common for us to say, "Christianity doesn't work for me."

God's desire is for us to get real with others and Him on the basis of a heart-to-heart relationship. This means that we no longer have to buck heads intellectually through the mind and the emotions with each other; rather we're able to extend our attitudes toward each other and communicate with each other with love and affection through the heart, the inner person or the control center of our lives. The heart is that spirit deep within us that connects us with God. When we live the Christian life through this heart-to-heart principle, we will find that our confidence level in ourselves and in God will increase. We therefore will gain the expectation that God's promises are real not only on paper but also in our lives; however, if we choose to continue on the devastating path of a head-to-head approach, our confidence will falter, and we will experience the wretchedness the apostle Paul experienced in his life.

Facing Christianity's Ebb and Flow

Have you ever experienced what seems to be a dichotomy in the Christian life? Have you sensed that inward challenge, a battle the Bible speaks of as a raging war in your heart? Often it may seem as though you are engaged in an intense, personal struggle deep in your soul. On the other hand, there may be occasions when you find you are in an outward struggle with individuals who are within your sphere of relationships. When you experience either of these two struggles in your life, your confidence in Christianity may suddenly become shaky, as if your Christian foundation is about to crumble.

When you transfer your life to the other side of the scales to get your life in balance, however, you will discover that Christianity is a wonderful source of life. It provides ability, stability, sensibility, and tranquility in your everyday living and relationships. It also provides you with correction, intention, and direction in your spiritual life. Rather than finding a battle raging in your life, you find that there is pleasure in the joy and peace of resting in the presence of Jesus Christ. What we sense in this dichotomous relationship with Christianity is a pulling and tugging at our lives, much like the motion of the mighty ocean as its tide comes in and goes out. This experience is called the "ebb and flow of Christianity."

In my eyes this ebb-and-flow experience seems necessary for us to advance in our spiritual lives. It can be a positive

A Collision

experience in our walk with God. There is no doubt that the apostle Paul was acquainted with this same pulling and tugging in his life. He readily admitted his lack of ability to comprehend what was happening. He spoke as if he were perplexed and inches from being defeated. Paul looked at the pulling and tugging in his life and said, "For what I am doing, I do not understand" (Rom. 7:15a NKJV). He went on to say, "For what I will to do, that I do not practice; but what I hate, that I do" (Rom. 7:15b NKJV). We should all be grateful that Paul was courageous and transparent enough to share with us his struggle in his Christian walk.

Often believers hide this struggle from other people simply because of their pride. They want others to see them as extremely spiritual people. Why do we desire to have others see us as spiritual giants when we know in our hearts that we're struggling? When we know this attitude can become a stumbling block in our lives, instead of hiding our faults, we should seek guidance and help so we can get back on the right path in our Christian walk.

Have you ever had this sense of defeat and despair in your Christian life? Maybe what you truly wanted to accomplish in your life wasn't happening. Maybe you were being pulled in the direction of something sinful and wrong — something you were against. In Romans 6:4, Paul described the victorious Christian life to us in terms of death, burial, and resurrection. "Therefore we were buried with Him through baptism into death, that just as Christ was raised from the dead by the glory of the Father, even so we also should walk in newness of life" (Rom. 6:4 NKJV).

The promise then is that today we can walk in the newness of life. We shouldn't continue to walk as old men or women or as the old people we once were. God has privileged us and challenged us through the Holy Spirit's enablement of us to walk in victory. We can no longer throw out the excuses we so often use as to why we're walking like old men or women. Excuses can include "This is just the way I am" or "This is how I grew up" or even "You don't know all the pain I've experienced in my life." Do any of these excuses sound familiar? We can find joy in the fact that we can be honest and open about the ebb and flow in our lives and quit making excuses.

Sometimes I find myself wondering whether Christianity can be authentic in my Christian life. Can and will it produce the effect on my life that it lays claim to in the word of God? My question is whether I can rely on the declaration in the Bible concerning the power of the resurrection of Jesus Christ. At times I wonder where this victory can be found, whether this victory I so often read about but seldom experience really exists.

Because of this Christian ebb and flow we encounter, I often feel like the apostle Peter when he and the disciples heard Jesus would be leaving this earth and helplessly realized they no longer would experience the physical presence of Jesus. Peter proclaimed, "I am going fishing." The rest of the disciples agreeably followed suit and said, "We're going with you." The disciples were simply saying, "We're going to go back to what we were doing before He came because this Christianity isn't going to work for us."

Two men were walking along the road to Emmaus with the resurrected Lord, though unknowingly, when the Lord said to them, "What kind of conversation is this that you have with one another as you walk and are sad?" (Luke 24:17 NKJV) The two men were thinking about the claims Jesus had made, and they likely believed those claims would not be fulfilled because someone had supposedly stolen the body of Christ. At this point in their lives, they weren't experiencing the victory the Lord had promised them.

Facing Truth in the Heart

The question we must answer in our lives is this: can we relate to the ebb and flow of Christianity and accept it in the way God intended for life to be? Or would we rather forget about it, sweep it under the carpet, and continue on with miserable dispositions and wretched lives? We can nonchalantly act as if turmoil isn't happening in our lives. When someone asks us how we're doing, we can give the typical reply and say everything is going great. The problem with this common response is that it's the usual Christian head-to-head answer and is very superficial. This answer doesn't come from the heart.

Are you willing to take time to reflect on your relationship with the Lord long enough to get real with yourself and with God? Are you willing to seek the truth and find peace in the midst of a raging war? Do you have the courage to be real and face the ebb and flow of Christianity?

You may be saying right this very minute, "No, that isn't true about me. I have God all figured out. My life is very linear — no ups or downs and no loops or twists for me to deal with." Let me ask you a question. How is this philosophy of life turning out for you? Do you have a great job and make a lot of money? Are you living in a beautiful home and driving an expensive car? Is your physical and mental health well? Did your children turn out the way you'd always planned? Are all your relationships running smoothly? Do you have any disappointments, discouragements, or disillusionments? Really? So everything is going as expected?

Some of you may say, "Yes, I know exactly what you're talking about, and you've described my life perfectly. The victorious Christian life is my heart's desire, but there are times when my relationships are like the ebb and flow of the ocean's tide. There are moments when I experience struggles in my life and other moments when I experience great peace." If this describes you, it's good that you're willing to cast aside superficial head-to-head answers and that you have the desire to be real and look at the heart of the matter.

Let me assure you that admitting this struggle may be exactly where God wants you to be at the present time, because it is here where you realize you must make some corrections in your life. We may fight these corrections, but they're exactly what we need for God to continue the great work He has begun in us.

Incidentally, to experience this struggle isn't at all unnatural according to the very essence of Christianity. I'm afraid some overzealous Bible teachers give a false sense of expectations; once you become a Christian, they say, you will never encounter these struggles. When those expectations aren't met, we begin to doubt whether Christianity really works. Christianity *does* work, and these struggles are various segments of our Christian-growth journey.

It was at such a point in his life when the apostle Paul said in Philippians 3:10–11, "That I may know Him, and the power of His resurrection, and the fellowship of His sufferings, being made conformable unto His death; if by any means I might attain to the resurrection of the dead." Paul wanted to know about God intellectually, but his greatest desire was to know God in his heart. He wanted a deep, intimate relationship with God.

How do we develop our lives so that we have a genuine, intimate relationship with God? So we can overcome the ebb and flow of Christianity and have lives that are pure, peaceable, gentle, and without hypocrisy? It involves getting out of our comfort zones and taking a journey that is exciting, encouraging, challenging, and life changing. This journey will give you a new perspective about yourself and your almighty God. Yes, you will see yourself as you've never seen yourself, and you will see God as you've never seen Him. It is an awesome journey to take!

Facing Life-Changing Decisions

I challenge you to take your spiritual life journey to a more profound level, a journey that is on the cutting edge of life, one that is similar to an outer-space, cutting-edge adventure, except yours will be an inner-space adventure. This journey has been called the eighteen-inch journey from the head to the heart. This journey will break you out of the known and comfortable life of Christianity and move you to a deeper, unknown, sometimes-uncomfortable life of abiding in Christ. When I say "unknown," I mean it is a path God knows but one still unknown to you because you have yet to travel down this road.

Jacob's life represents this God-seeking journey in the Book of Genesis. Jacob dealt with multiple life-altering struggles in his life. In fact we can see that most of his life was like an ebb and flow of Christianity. We can see his eighteen-inch journey from the head to the heart when he crossed the ford at Jabbok, sent his family over the brook, and was left alone with God. In that time of being alone with God, he wrestled with God in a hand-to-hand battle. He wasn't willing to turn God loose until God had blessed him by changing his life from a head-to-head, confrontational life to a heart-to-heart, tranquil life.

Jacob's journey is similar to where this journey can take you. Are there not times when you wish you had the courage to wrestle with God? And if you took that step, wouldn't you want to continue in that struggle until your life changed and you received the blessing and promises of God? Is it a rough journey? Yes. The

Bible states that Jacob came away limping from that encounter with God. Was the pain worth the journey? Yes. The Bible goes on to say in Genesis 32:30 that Jacob called the place Peniel, which means "for I have seen God face-to-face."

To take this rough-and-rocky eighteen-inch journey, which is filled with curves, hills, potholes, speed bumps, roadwork, and detours, we must first look at the reality of life and its disappointments and disillusionments. We're going to take a good look at what, I believe, many of us have or will experience over the course of our spiritual journey, and it is filled with painful conflict and destructive strife. Conflict and strife cause frustrating circumstances to take place in our relationships at home, at school, at work, in the neighborhood, and at church. Most people don't want to deal with conflict and strife in their lives but often find it is there to deal with on a daily basis.

This book is about finding authentic Christianity and making it real in our spiritual walk with God. It is about reducing conflict and strife in our lives and replacing it with the peace and tranquility of God. It is about answering the question "Does Christianity work?" Most important, it is about finding victory in our walk with our Lord and Savior, Jesus Christ.

This magnificent journey I've spoken about can begin right now. Are you ready to face the ebb and flow of Christianity? Are you ready to face the truth and make a life-changing decision in your heart? Are you ready to experience God as you've never experienced Him before? What do you say? Let's get started! Keep in mind that there will always be another intersection we must cross in the journey of life.

Chapter 2

A Clash

A Clash at the Main Intersection of Life
Why Is There Strife in Our Lives?

He that is of a proud heart stirreth up strife.
—Prov. 28:25a

When good people have a falling out, only one of them may be at fault; but if the strife continues long, usually both become guilty.
—Thomas Fuller

If we open a quarrel between the past and the present, we shall find that we have lost the future.
—Winston Churchill

Each party needs the opportunity to voice fears, hurts, and concerns. We clear the weeds of our hearts by naming, admitting, and talking about them. So often our wars are based on misinformation, misconceptions, and misunderstanding. The experience of being heard and understood is the furrow into which the seeds of love can later be sown.
—St. Francis of Assisi

I experienced a collision at the corner of Christianity and life. It was a personal conflict I had in terms of questioning the power and influence of Christianity and why it wasn't working in my life. To add insult to injury, I soon found myself a few blocks down the highway, having a clash at the main intersection of my life as I dealt with all the strife in my personal relationships. "Why is there strife in our lives?" was the new question I knew must be answered if I were to progress further in my spiritual life.

The author of the Book of Proverbs brings us straight to the heart of the matter concerning strife. The head hasn't yet transferred its knowledge to the heart; therefore the heart becomes proud. It is a proud heart that stirs up strife, according to our Scripture. If we're committed to everyday, head-to-head living in our spiritual lives and aren't willing to move to the heart-to-heart principle of living, then the fruit of strife, rather than the fruit of the Spirit, will be produced in all our relationships.

In a moment we're going to become fruit inspectors so we can get a glimpse of the effects of strife in our various relationships: in our families, in education, in government, in religion, and within ourselves. Before we can begin our spiritual heart journey, we'll have to face some things and see why we have so much conflict in our culture today.

The Meaning of Strife

To assist us in our understanding of strife, we must first define exactly what the word *strife* means. Some words, such as *love*, are hard to define, and it's difficult to grasp their meaning. For instance if we truly love someone, we know the feeling of this love, but to put it into words so someone else can understand our feeling is almost impossible. *Strife* isn't a hard word to define; we know exactly what it means and how to define it.

Webster's New World College Dictionary defines *strife* as "the act of striving or vying with another, a bitter fighting and quarreling."[1] The Hebrew and Greek languages define *strife* as a contest, with quarreling, discord, contention, and wrangling. All of us know exactly what strife means and how it feels.

The Meaning of "Stirreth Up"

At the end of Proverbs 28:25a, we see the phrase "stirreth up strife." The word *stirreth* means to grate or grind into shreds by rubbing and scraping. A great visual example of *stirreth* is cheese being grated, with bits and pieces flying in all directions.

For me a more personal example of the word *stirreth* would be when I was a child growing up on a farm. Occasionally I had the misfortune of stirring up a hornets' nest. It was a terrible scene, with hornets flying in every direction and me sprinting as fast as I could. I quickly learned that I couldn't run as fast as an angry hornet could fly; consequently one or more of the hornets eventually stung me. I can still remember the dreadful pain of a hornet's stinger in my body, and the problem had occurred because I'd stirred up a hornets' nest.

I imagine that most of us have witnessed such an instance in our families, at our workplace, and most likely in our church. Maybe someone in your midst stirred up strife by allowing words and emotions to fly in all directions, and as the result of his or her actions, you may still carry the stinger and experience the pain of that strife today.

Strife and discord aren't new to the postmodern Christian experience. In fact both occur very early in the word of God. We can see their origin with Lucifer in Isaiah 14:13, when he thought in his heart, "For thou hast said in thine heart, I will ascend into

---

1 *Webster's New World College Dictionary,* 4th edition, Wiley Publishing

heaven, I will exalt my throne above the stars of God: I will sit also upon the mount of the congregation, in the sides of the north." There has been strife between Satan and God ever since that fateful day. Satan took that same attitude of pride into the Garden of Eden when he tempted Adam and Eve to disobey God. That is when strife and discord became an integral part of the human experience. Students of history can follow the trail of strife into every era of human existence. Multitudes of people have died, been maimed, or left behind in psychological ruins due to strife. There hasn't been a generation of people who have escaped its terror on their secular or religious lives.

What does this strife look like? What should we look for to tell whether this is the reality of our lives? What are the indicators that warn us that we're involved in strife with other people? We all have numerous spheres of relationships we have entered into and developed. We will look at a few of these relationships to see how they measure up. As we look at these relationships, you will immediately see the ebb and flow of Christianity being created if you are resolved to continue a head-to-head relationship rather than a heart-to-heart relationship.

How Does Strife Affect Our Families?

Areas of Strife in Our Families

Strife can usually be found in a few basic areas in our families. A husband and wife may disagree about matters relating to their roles in the marriage, about how to raise their children, about managing their finances, or even about the type of permissible entertainment. Often there may be a great gulf between their levels of individual spirituality.

Strife is often the result of unfulfilled expectations, controlling parents or in-laws, or little to no communication. Not only can there be strife with the spouse, but there often are confrontational moments with our children when they are disobedient, disrespectful, and disagreeable.

Attitudes of Strife in Our Minds
If we allow strife to continue for a prolonged period of time in these areas of our family lives, we will begin to see a trend developing in our attitudes. We may become argumentative, irritable, and often extremely angry at the slightest offense. Our head-to-head communication begins to break down, and instead of having a normal conversation with our spouse or child, we yell or give him or her the cold shoulder. We hold on to an attitude that we know we're right and that we aren't the ones who need to change.

Actions of Strife in Our Behavior
Attitudes usually produce actions, and those actions can be devastating. When strife reaches a point of no return, the process of closing our spirit to the other person begins to take place. We may be connected intellectually to that person, but inwardly we are disconnected. We may respond with words, but there is absolutely no response with our feelings. We're no longer open to our spouse or child. This closed spirit more than likely will produce a marriage that is seen as structural but isn't a functional marriage, or often it will produce a divorce. Intimacy within the relationship will become strained or eventually become a thing of the past. Our children will look forward to the day when they can move out and get away from living a life of hell.

What I just described is the fruit of a head-to-head relationship that stirs up strife in our homes.

How Does Strife Affect Our Churches?

Areas of Strife in Our Churches

The church of Jesus Christ isn't immune to strife. We see it in epidemic forms as each generation jockeys for position and power in the church. Allow me to list the areas in which strife is predominant in our churches. We can see it in the manner in which we conduct our worship services and in the music we sing. Are hymns the only spiritual songs accepted, or are contemporary songs the only music allowed? Has each side drawn a line in the sand so that consequently every Sunday there is strife in our worship services?

In the message presented, which versions of the Bible are accepted? Will the method of preaching the sermon be delivered from behind the pulpit or in a contemporary style? Will the pastor or deacons or both lead the management of the church? Who in the church determines the expenditures of funds received? Who decides the modesty or style of clothing worn to the services? Are suits the only attire permitted for men, or can they dress more casually? Are ladies allowed to only wear dresses, or are they permitted to wear slacks? Is the strife caused by the church's members or by its leaders?

Attitudes of Strife in the Mind

Because we have differing opinions in these various areas, confrontations may occur if our differing is done in a head-to-head manner. Sides will develop over the issues, and so will attitudes. Some of the arguments may include the following: "I will not listen to you because I have more important things to say"; "My preference is always right"; "I am more spiritual than you"; "I belonged to this church first, so I get my way"; "I'm the pastor, so I get to tell everyone what to do"; "I'm traditional, or I'm contemporary, and I'm not going to change, and if I can't have it my way, I'll just leave." Many people hold on to the attitude that the issue is all about them, their needs, and their wants. Pastors as well may have the attitude of "It's my way or the highway." You may be familiar with some of these attitudes in many churches today.

Actions of Strife in Our Behavior

Once again attitudes are followed by actions. Today people are hopping from one church to another at the speed of light. Character assassination has become a spiritual sport, and gossiping is a well-oiled activity among Christians and church leaders. Being meanspirited seems to be more in vogue than being filled with God's Spirit. Outbursts of anger are often tolerated in our circles. The Christian principle of forgiveness is almost a lost art in our churches.

What I have just described is the fruit of a head-to-head relationship that stirs up strife in our churches. As you know, this same principle applies to our relationships at work, at school, and with our neighbors. "He that is of a proud heart stirreth up strife" (Prov. 28:25a). The examples given can provide us with a picture of what strife looks like and why it happens in our relationships. They can also give us an incentive to purge strife from our lives as much as possible.

Does Christianity Work in Your Family or Church?

We now come back to the question presented in chapter one. Does Christianity work? Yes, it does. Christianity has to work because Paul said, "being confident of this very thing, that he which hath begun a good work in you will perform it until the day of Jesus Christ" (Phil. 1:6). But that isn't all; Paul went on to say, "For it is God which worketh in you both to will and to do of his good pleasure" (Phil. 2:13).

Why then does Christianity break down? It breaks down because Christianity is a journey — a long journey — and there are many legs to that journey that bring us to a place of transformation. It breaks down because we haven't yet reached the point where we appropriate and assimilate the word of God into our hearts. The eighteen-inch journey from the head to the heart hasn't yet taken place in our lives. To "appropriate" means to take possession of the word of God and claim it for our lives. To "assimilate" means to absorb the word of God to grow spiritually, much like we absorb nutrients from food into the cells and tissues of our bodies to grow physically. I discuss assimilation and appropriation in depth in a later chapter.

We have to let go and let God be in control of our lives. One reason our lives become overwhelmed with strife is because we're so task oriented. We spend most of our time performing for God by doing great and admirable acts. Yet we overlook the fact that God is more interested in our growth and in what we become rather than in what we do. God knows that if we would become what He has in mind for us, then our *doing* would automatically flow from our lives similar to how water and nutrients flowing through a tree produce fruit. *Becoming* is accomplished through the appropriation and assimilation of the word of God.

The reason our families and churches are so splintered today is because we deal with each other in a head-to-head manner. Once again, a head-to-head relationship is one that is confrontational and superficial. The focus of this book is to lead us to that

A Clash

deeper spiritual life in which we will be able to build our relationships on a heart-to-heart basis. Very seldom do we have the courage to speak to each other in the spiritual heart-to-heart language. That's because doing so and living in that realm would more than likely expose us for what we really are, and that thought scares us to death.

If we choose to appropriate and assimilate the knowledge we have in our heads to our hearts, our lives will change dramatically. Instead of suffering the constant pain and agony of strife, we will experience tranquility, joy, and the peace of God, which surpasses all understanding. At some point we will joyfully find ourselves saying, "Hey, this really does work."

Having spent some time getting a snapshot view of how strife looks, we also need to get a glimpse of the personal characteristics that drive someone to strife. Maybe we need to get a mirror handy and take a good, long, deep look at our spiritual lives and ask ourselves a simple question: "Is it me, Lord, who is causing the strife in my relationships?"

With all the collisions and the clashes I experienced at almost every intersection of my Christian life, I became a little paranoid about what was happening. When I entered every intersection of my life, I came almost to a complete stop and looked around to see who was lurking around the next corner, ready to broadside me and knock me off the path of spiritual growth. Guess what? I found the culprit. In the next chapter, I expose the culprit and pull him out in the open for everyone to see.

Chapter 3
A Culprit

*A Conspirator Lurking in Every
Neighborhood of Life
Who Causes the Strife?*

Hatred stirs up strife, but love covers all offenses.
—Prov. 10:12 ESV

A careless word may kindle strife; a cruel word may wreck a life; a timely word may level stress; a loving word may heal and bless.
—unknown

As soon as I identified the culprit that had broadsided me at every corner of my life, I came to realize the conspirator had lived in my neighborhood all along. Actually, while living in the information age with so much technology available to me, how could I have missed the culprit? You see, the culprit that causes so much strife in our lives is very identifiable. We'll look at the culprit's identity in this chapter.

Who, then, are these people who cause strife, and what are their characteristics? What do they look like, and how do they act? What kind of attitudes do they carry around with them? We could all define in our own opinions the characteristics of such people, but these opinions would be tainted by our own biases. Previously we glanced at their attitudes and actions, which are exposed for everyone to see. We want to look deeper into the issue to get a grasp on the source of strife and what motivates such behavior. What I do know is that the Bible speaks of the issue and teaches that the source is from the heart and that the motivation is from a proud heart.

Remember, life is lived from the heart, "for out of it spring the issues of life" (Prov. 4:23b NKJV). Before we can begin our journey, allowing God to transform our hearts, we must first have an understanding of the heart and its attitude, its actions, and how it needs to be tended if Christianity is to work in our lives.

The issue of strife is of great importance to God. He doesn't pull any punches; He makes it crystal clear what kind of person "stirreth up strife." As you read the following list of traits that define a person who "stirreth up strife," you will be able to see more clearly why we sometimes question Christianity. You will also gain a greater understanding of why there is strife in Christianity and all our relationships.

What we observe from the attitudes and actions of those who cause strife is that these people live Christianity from a confrontational, head-to-head approach and therefore produce strife in their relationships. These individuals have received and assimilated information and knowledge from the Bible and have stored it in their heads. But they haven't yet taken the eighteen-inch journey to transfer that information and knowledge from their heads to their hearts. This step would enable them to eliminate strife from their lives through a heart-to-heart approach to life.

Since they haven't yet made this journey, their hearts aren't yet engaged in their relationships. As we glance at the list of biblical characteristics of a heart filled with strife, I'm certain that most of us will be able to relate to at least a couple of them. Some characteristics may stand out because we encountered them in previous experiences that have been resolved, while others may still be part of our lives.

Keep in mind that the following characteristics discussed in this chapter originates from the heart and mind of God. We should take heed of what God says about strife.

A Proud Person

He that is of a proud heart stirreth up strife.
—Prov. 28:25a

He is proud, knowing nothing, but doting about questions and strifes of words, whereof cometh envy, strife, railings, evil surmisings.
—1 Tim. 6:4

Pride goeth before destruction and a haughty spirit before a fall.
—Prov. 16:18

According to our Scripture, a proud person is an egotistical person. One of the ultimate causes of strife is pride. The definition of a prideful person is someone who is inflated, lifted up, and truly believes he or she is better than others. Proud people are those who overvalue themselves and trust in their own knowledge, wisdom, and strength. Somewhere along the way, they will stumble and fall in their relationships.

An Angry Person

An angry man stirreth up strife.
—Prov. 29:22

An angry person is a wounded person. Have you ever come across an angry person? More often than not, angry people are those who have been hurt in a relationship. There isn't enough room to list the countless ways they could have been wounded, but the hurt they feel in their hearts is real, and that hurt causes anger. Hurting people hurt people. Why? They unintentionally hurt others because they haven't dealt with their own wounds, nor have they sought forgiveness. To sweep their pain under the carpet, they transfer that hurt to others. Because of this, they continue to live with anger, and as it has been said, an angry person "stirreth up strife."

A Talebearer

Where there is no wood, the fire goes out; and where there is no talebearer, strife ceases.
—Prov. 26:20 NKJV

A talebearer is someone who gossips. A fire must have fuel to burn. If there is no fuel, the fire goes out. Gossip is a natural fuel that stirs up strife. A talebearer plays a role as a person who spreads malicious rumors about others. Gossip is one of the greatest examples of what a superficial head-to-head relationship will produce. A person who has made the journey from the head to the heart will know that gossip is indeed a sin, and therefore strife will cease in his or her life.

A Contentious Person

As coals are to burning coals, and wood to fire; so is a contentious man to kindle strife.
—Prov. 26:21

A perverse man sows strife, and a whisperer separates the best of friends.
—Prov. 16:28 NKJV

A contentious person is one who originates quarrels. The contentious man's tongue is set ablaze, allowing him to set fire to the whole community in which he dwells. This man is controversial, argumentative, and touchy. A contentious person will make arguable statements that will cause you to question someone's actions in order to provoke friction between you and that person. Some people feel as if they must have some type of contention going on in their lives at all times. If they don't have this, they will find a way to create contention and discord.

A Carnal Person

Now the works of the flesh are manifest, which are these; adultery, fornication, uncleanness, lasciviousness, idolatry, witchcraft, hatred, variance, emulations, wrath, strife, seditions, heresies, envyings, murderers, drunkenness, revellings, and such like: of the which I tell you before, as I have also told you in time past, that they which do such things shall not inherit the kingdom of God.
—Gal. 5:19-21

For ye are yet carnal: for whereas there is among you envying, and strife, and divisions, are ye not carnal, and walk as men?
—*1 Cor. 3:3*

A carnal person is one who lacks spiritual maturity. The apostle Paul was surprised that the Christians in Corinth hadn't yet blossomed into mature believers. The relationships within the Corinthian church are a prime example of a head-to-head relationship, which is very similar to what we see in our churches today. Paul made it clear that their carnality was causing strife in the church. Head-to-head relationships are developed through carnality. Heart-to-heart relationships are developed through Holy Spirit empowerment.

Let me share a word of encouragement to new and young believers in the Lord. Christianity is a lifelong journey. When we're born again through Christ Jesus, we begin the journey as little babies in our spiritual lives. Building our relationships on a head-to-head basis comes naturally to us. However, as we grow and mature in our spiritual walk with Christ, our biblical knowledge gradually begins to make that eighteen-inch transfer from our heads to our hearts. As it does, we may find that we can and will nurture all of our relationships on a heart-to-heart basis. As we keep this in mind, we can truly live a life without all the contention and strife I've been talking about. Be encouraged, for you can live in victory, not defeat.

Now that we've given consideration to the dilemma of strife in our lives, we'll want to gradually move toward answering the question of whether Christianity really does work. We're going to prepare for a surgical procedure on our spiritual hearts. This procedure is much like that of a surgeon preparing to perform heart surgery on his or her patient's physical heart. God created us and blessed us with a physical heart and a spiritual heart. Everyone knows the purpose of our physical hearts, but not everyone understands the importance and meaning of our spiritual hearts. Scholars speak of the spiritual heart as being the inner person, the center of spiritual activity that provides the operations of human life and spiritual life in our relationship with God.

Let me challenge you to read the remaining chapters of this book carefully. We're going to take a hard look at the interior of our lives, the parts of our lives that are spiritual and so difficult for us to understand. This is the intangible part of life; we know it's there, but we cannot grasp its meaning because we cannot touch it like we can touch physical matter.

We're also going to dig deep into Scripture to see what God has to say about every aspect of the spiritual heart and how that heart influences and affects our daily lives. Only then will we come to realize why God says we shouldn't look down on and judge those around us based on their outside appearance.

Now I want to share with you the clue that got me back on the highway of life. If you've experienced being broadsided and knocked off the highway of life, this clue will help you get back on your spiritual journey and move you on down the road to experience the beauty God has in store for you. Believe me, it's a great journey.

Chapter 4
A Clue

*Getting You Back on the Highway of Life
How Does Christianity Work?*

And be renewed in the spirit *of your* mind.
—*Eph. 4:23 (emphasis added)*

And he that searcheth the hearts knoweth what is the mind *of the* Spirit*, because he maketh intercession for the saints according to the will of God.*
—*Rom. 8:27 (emphasis added)*

Being confident of this very thing, that he which hath begun a good work in you will perform it until the day of Jesus Christ.
—*Phil. 1:6*

    One of the reasons we find ourselves in the junk pile of Christianity is because we may have a reservoir of information in our minds about the Bible, but we're clueless as to how to apply it to our lives. For us to meander our way through our spiritual lives without having a wreck at every intersection, it's important that we find the clue that will aid us in explaining the answers to our most difficult questions. Here is the clue that will unlock the biblical formula for spiritual growth and keep us on the journey without being involved in wreck after wreck.
    Andrew Murray, a teacher, writer, and missionary working in South Africa in the late 1800's, believed that God does not ask

you to give the perfect surrender of your life in your strength, or by the power of your will; God is willing to work it in you. Do we not read the following in the Bible? "For it is God which worketh in you both to will and to do of His good pleasure" (Phil. 2:13).

Who Has the Answer?

The one question I've been asked more than any other during the many years I have been in full-time ministry is "How does Christianity work?" I believe Christians, more often than not, have a longing to live their lives in accordance with the word of God. When they exercise their faith according to biblical principle, they desire to see that principle carried out in their daily lives.

As we receive knowledge from the word of God through many different channels — such as reading the Bible, hearing it over the radio, watching it on television, receiving it through our iPhones or iPads, attending Bible classes, or hearing a sermon on Sunday morning — we actually begin the process of applying that knowledge to our lives. We naturally expect the word of God to take effect immediately and manifest itself in our daily lives. At some point a situation may arise, such as in our marriage, in which we depend on and expect a certain biblical principle to perform in our lives. If and when it doesn't perform because of that situation, we start to question ourselves and possibly begin to experience the ebb and flow of Christianity.

Maybe for some unexpected reason, the seed of that principle didn't germinate in our hearts; therefore the expected outcome didn't occur. Now, when we find ourselves in this barren condition, we pose questions such as the following: "How does it work?" "How can Christianity truly become a reality in my life?"

A Clue

or "What is necessary for me to do to see this principle developed in my life?" Often we ask, "Who can give me an answer to these questions?"

I'm not sure whether any human being can answer these questions to our satisfaction. In fact it's likely that God is the only one who can truly answer these questions for you. I know there have been multiple times in my life when I asked myself many of these same questions. Perhaps you've faced some of these questions throughout your own life. Maybe right now you're in a spiritual drought, asking, "How does Christianity work for me?"

One thing I enjoy about having a relationship with God is that we don't always need all the answers to all the spiritual questions we may have. It's ridiculous for us to think we deserve an answer from almighty God to every question. I also find it amazing and somewhat astonishing that we can read, study, memorize, dissect, and analyze the Bible to come up with all the answers to our denominational doctrines, creeds, and codes of conduct — yet when it comes to seeing how a principle in the word of God can take root in our lives, for us to become fruitful through that principle, we somehow get totally lost and confused. The only words we can muster up at that point are "How does Christianity work?" The reason we're confused is that the doctrines, creeds, and codes of conduct relate to the thinking of our minds, but the question of how Christianity works in our lives relates to the actions of our hearts.

I will make an attempt to answer, to a certain degree of satisfaction, the question "How does Christianity work?" In fact discovering and understanding the answer to this vital question becomes the pivotal element of the eighteen-inch journey from the head to the heart if that spiritual journey is to be a successful one. We're going to look at the God-given blueprint for transferring information from our minds to our hearts so we may be transformed into the loving and compassionate image of Jesus Christ.

Transformed by the Renewing of Our Minds

We will begin our quest in Romans 12:2. In this passage Paul challenged believers in Rome not to be conformed to the world but to be transformed by the renewing of their minds. He told them that the world is not the image you should be producing or portraying. In that verse he continued to say that we must be transformed. In other words we should make a change in our minds that will change our lives and images. Thus our behavior will be different from what this world and culture view as normal. This may sound simple, but how do you make a change in your mind and your image? Paul went on to provide the answer to that question by declaring, "By the renewing of your mind." What Paul was speaking of is a spiritual, metamorphic process that takes place from our minds to our hearts. This process will change us from the worldly head-to-head image to a Christlike heart-to-heart image.

Now there is another question that rises upon the scene. What is the course of action we should take to renew our minds? Paul knew his subject matter well; he had lived through this transformation, and he didn't leave us hanging in confusion. He provided us with the biblical answers to this agonizing question. Therefore we will continue our thought process and allow his answers to unfold within our hearts. Please closely note the breakdown of our heart management — control by the spirit of the mind or control by the mind of the Spirit.

Heart Management: Spirit of the Mind
What Does This Life Look Like?

To understand what the Christian life looks like, we must understand and implement what I call "heart management." Either we're going to manage our hearts through the spirit of the mind or allow God to manage our hearts through the mind of the Spirit. Make no mistake about it; the heart must be managed, "for out of it are the issues of life" (Prov. 4:23).

The spirit of the mind gives direction and manages the information being transferred from our minds to our hearts, according to the following Scripture:

> This I say therefore, and testify in the Lord, that ye henceforth walk not as other Gentiles walk, in the vanity of their mind, Having the understanding darkened, being alienated from the life of God through the ignorance that is in them, because of the blindness of their heart: Who being past feeling have given themselves over unto lasciviousness, to work all uncleanness with greediness. But ye have not so learned Christ; If so be that ye have heard him, and have been taught by him, as the truth is in Jesus: That ye put off concerning the former conversation the old man, which is corrupt according to the deceitful lust; *And be renewed in the spirit of your mind*; And that ye put on the new man, which after God is created in righteousness and true holiness. (Eph. 4:17–24, emphasis added)

The Holy Potholes of Christianity

In the first part of this short passage of Scripture, Paul described a head-to-head confrontational lifestyle, which causes a lot of the strife I discussed in previous chapters. Notice he described an image the world produces through its culture. We aren't to be conformed to that image: futility of the mind, a darkened understanding, alienation from the life of God, ignorance, blindness of the heart, lewdness, uncleanness, and greediness. These characteristics define the "old man" we were before we came to know Jesus Christ as our personal Lord and Savior. This image is neither who we are at the present time nor what we should look like as Christians.

Kenneth Wuest comments on Ephesians 4:23, saying, "The spirit is the human spirit, having its seat and directing the mind."[2] The NIV translation of Ephesians 4:23 says, "To be made new in the *attitude* of your minds" (emphasis added). Basically what this verse says is that our minds have a spirit of their own. That spirit has its own outlook, perspective, opinion, approach, and position in all matters, such as what constitutes marriage, the roles in marriage, the raising of children, the handling of money, and all the social issues our culture puts forth, including politics, religion, and many other areas in which we experience conflict.

In other words your spirit has its own fixed mental attitude. With this attitude the spirit of your mind directs information to your heart. Your heart will respond accordingly and issue forth its behavior, following the dictates of the spirit of your mind. This is the reason we Christians approach life like the world does, in a head-to-head manner. The spirit of our minds constantly directs us, and our hearts responds to that direction. Let me prove this claim with an example from the word of God: "Let no corrupt communication

---

2 *Weust's Word Studies in the Greek New Testament* (four-volume set), Kenneth S. Wuest, Eerdmans, 1961

proceed out of your mouth, but that which is good to the use of edifying, that it may minister grace unto the hearers" (Eph. 4:29).

Now imagine that you're with a group of people and that your conversation has become centered on gossip about a person who isn't present. You know the word of God is very explicit about what comes out of our mouths. You may not feel comfortable being in this situation, but all the while your head — the spirit of your mind — sends information to your heart. Because the spirit of your mind is in control, it may try to tell you, "It's OK. Go ahead and continue to gossip," or it might even say, "God will understand. Don't worry about it. He or she had it coming anyway." The spirit of your mind wants you to think this gossip isn't a big deal. We continually find ourselves allowing the spirit of the mind to govern our lives. Consequently this behavior of gossip will produce strife in our lives.

Heart Management: Mind of the Spirit
What Does This Life Look Like?

The *mind* of the *Spirit* yearns to override the *spirit* of the *mind* and wants to give direction and manage the information that is being transferred from our minds to our hearts. Paul described the new man as follows: "And be renewed in the spirit of your mind; and that ye put on the new man, which after God is created in righteousness and true holiness" (Eph. 4:23-24). These verses describe a new image, a heart-to-heart, Christ-centered life, which is the very source of our being able to live in tranquility through righteousness and holiness.

When we look closer at God's blueprint, we find that God never intended for us to live according to the spirit of the mind. His plan is for us to live according to the mind of the Spirit. "Likewise the Spirit also helpeth our infirmities: for we know not what we should pray for as we ought: but the Spirit itself maketh intercession for us with groanings which cannot be uttered. And he that searcheth the hearts knoweth what is the *mind of the Spirit*, because he maketh intercession for the saints according to the will of God" (Rom. 8:26–27, emphasis added).

God searches your heart, not to know what your conscious prayers are, but to find out what the prayer of the Holy Spirit is in your life. In this way God searches the mind of the Spirit. Not only is God searching the mind of the Spirit to see what the Holy Spirit is praying, but the Holy Spirit is also praying and directing the spirit of your mind to be obedient to the will of God.

We need to allow the mind of the Spirit of God to override the spirit of our mind for us to be transformed by the renewing of our minds according to God's word. In fact this step runs to the very core of our making the eighteen-inch journey from the head to the heart. When the spirit of our mind is renewed by the mind of the Holy Spirit, then and only then will the Holy Spirit send a message to our hearts, and our hearts will respond to God's will, and our images will be transformed.

Let's take a step back to the example about gossip. The spirit of the mind will flash a green light our way and tell our minds, "It's OK. You can continue in this sin." At the same time, the mind of the Spirit will flash a red light and tell our hearts to do the exact opposite. It will let our hearts know that this behavior isn't according to the will of God, persuading us to stop the gossip. The Holy Spirit will say that continuing in this sin isn't OK. In doing so the mind of the Holy Spirit will convict us. At this point we will have to make a choice, either to excuse ourselves from the conversation and tell the people involved that this behavior is wrong or to continue in our sin.

The Holy Spirit's "Outside In" and "Inside Out" Management

Being confident of this very thing, that he which hath begun a good work in you will perform it until the day of Jesus Christ.
—Phil. 1:6

For it is God which worketh in you both to will and to do of his good pleasure.
—Phil. 2:13

    Religious scholars call this the working *into* and working *out of* our lives by the Holy Spirit. The Holy Spirit inspired holy men of old to write the word of God. As we read the word of God, the Holy Spirit illuminates our minds to understand the words He inspired men to write. The Holy Spirit plants God's word in our minds and overrides the spirit of our minds so His word may be transferred into our hearts. This way our hearts can respond according to the will of God. Then the Holy Spirit's power invigorates our hearts to work out of our lives what He has worked into our lives. When this happens, we have become the channel for the fruit of the Spirit to flow freely from our lives, or as the apostle John stated, "He that believeth on me, as the Scripture hath said, out of his belly shall flow rivers of living water" (John 7:38). In comparison to a worldly Dead Sea image, in which our lives are stagnant, our image, which has been transformed, is now pictured as a flowing river of living water.
    In place of a head-to-head confrontational life, which is filled with constant strife, we now can experience a heart-to-heart life filled with calmness, peace, and tranquility.

The apostle Paul's formula or blueprint to the question "How does Christianity work?" is clear, now that we're transformed by renewing the spirit of our minds with the mind of the Spirit. In other words we should allow the mind of the Holy Spirit to override the spirit of our minds so that the Holy Spirit can work *out of* us the fruit of the Spirit He is working *in* us.

Spiritual change is a process, and seeing its fruition takes time. The journey moves along slowly, one inch at a time, until we finalize the eighteen-inch, head-to-heart journey. In the following chapters, we will watch this eighteen-inch metamorphosis take place. Each step in the journey will be much like those of a cocoon turning into a butterfly, for we will see our hearts change from corrupt hearts to clean hearts.

What Does God See?

For the Lord seeth not as man seeth; for man looketh on the outward appearance, but the Lord looketh on the heart.
—1 Sam. 16:7b

The Bible clearly states that when God looks at us, He looks within us and sees our spiritual hearts. While people may look on the outward individual, God looks on the inward individual. So the question is "What does He see?" In the following chapters, we'll take a long, profound look into the spiritual heart of human beings as Scripture describes it in many ways. In a sense we could say we're going to conduct a spiritual health exam to determine the condition of our hearts in a way that's very similar to going to our doctor and getting a physical checkup.

The Bible lists descriptions for a variety of heart conditions. No doubt nestled somewhere in that list of conditions,

A Clue

the condition of our own spiritual hearts will be found there. According to the Bible, whatever spiritual condition we're currently inhabiting is the one God sees when He looks at our hearts. Yes, He does see us in whatever stage of heart condition we're presently in, even though we may try to hide it from others.

Now, if people look at a person's outward appearance, they will see something different from what God would see, because God looks only at our hearts. A person may look at someone's outward appearance and think that person is very spiritual because he or she practices all the spiritual disciplines, when in fact that person may not be spiritual in his or her heart at all.

However, the eyes of God on us are more important than the eyes of people. If we could take a step back and realize how concerned God is about the condition of our hearts, I believe we would have more of a desire to allow Him to change our hearts. Consequently, not only would others see us as spiritual beings from an outside appearance, but there would be a higher probability that God would see us as spiritual beings on the inside.

In previous chapters I discussed why the conflict in our Christian walk usually flows into every relationship we have and how it affects those relationships in different ways. We came to the conclusion that conflict in our families, workplaces, and churches can be traced back to the poor spiritual condition of our hearts. From our unclean hearts, unclean behavior pours out into every relationship we have in a head-to-head, confrontational lifestyle. Our focus has been to take a journey — an eighteen-inch journey — from our heads to our hearts and to find uplifting ways to enable us to accomplish this journey.

In upcoming chapters we'll take a journey through the assortment of heart conditions God reveals to us through Scripture. We will be able to find where our hearts are spiritually and truly examine our heart conditions to determine whether we are satisfied with that spiritual state. We will see whether we want to remain in the condition we're in at the present time or whether we want to make a change and take an alternate path. Looking at the menu of heart conditions, we may decide that we aren't at all satisfied with our current heart condition. This is when we may decide to allow God to begin to change our hearts into ones that are more at peace with ourselves, with the people around us, and with God.

Keep in mind that as we probe and dissect each heart condition, we will be looking at the very same thing God is looking at in our hearts and has been looking at with His own eyes for some time. Whatever heart condition describes you, please bear in mind that your heart will produce an attitude and action in accordance with that heart condition. Each heart condition produces its own fruit, which could be conflict, indifference, or if the heart is in the right place, peace. God will be the one to determine which it will be, because He knows the heart is producing it, "for out of it are the issues of life" (Prov. 4:23b) "for it is God which worketh in you both to will and to do of His good pleasure" (Phil. 2:13).

Let's begin the heart journey, traveling from location to location or, in other words, from one heart condition to another heart condition. At times the scenery will be dull, drab, dark, and rather boring. At other times the heart locations will have sceneries that are bright, fresh, and colorful.

Let's jump into our spiritual cars, go full speed ahead, and take a journey across the spiritual landscape of our lives. You

A Clue

now have the clue that will give you the answers to the spiritual-growth formula you've possibly been searching for in various places for years. Let the acceleration begin!

Let's journey from the head to the heart and from the control by the spirit of the mind to the control by the mind of the Spirit.

Part 2
Learn to Navigate

Driving through the Potholes

    I'm glad God provided us with the Bible. It is His road map and His directions for us to live the Christian life. It is vital that we read the Bible to find directions for where we should go in our journey. A navigator must have a map and a plan so that he or she will be successful in his or her journey.

    In the following chapters, we'll navigate through the various characteristics and conditions of the spiritual heart. With the map in hand, we'll learn how to drive through the potholes of life. The more we learn and know about the potholes, the more we'll be able to drive through them without a catastrophe.

    In our journey with God, the heart needs to be directed and ultimately changed. God looks on the heart of man and knows who is driving the heart. Now we must open the Scriptures to learn how to bring the heart to a place where it can navigate and drive through these potholes successfully.

Chapter 5
A Corrupt Heart

And I will give them one heart, and I will put a new spirit within you; and I will take the stony heart out of their flesh, and will give them a heart of flesh.
—Ezek. 11:19 (emphasis added)

He has said in his heart, I shall not be moved.
—Ps. 10:6a

If you live in the graveyard too long, you stop crying when someone dies.
—unknown

Worse than a bloody hand is a hard heart.
—Percy Bysshe Shelley

    We're packed and ready to go, so let's begin the journey of the heart. We're going to drive right into what the Bible calls a "corrupt heart." As we go through this portion of our spiritual journey, we will travel with our headlights on, because it's going to be a dark and dreary road. With this darkened heart, seeing the spiritual road we're traveling on will be hard.

    The condition of this particular corrupt heart is why there are so many spiritual accidents on this road. While we travel on this leg of the journey, there are so many possibilities of driving off the road and into the ditch and overturning our spiritual vehicle called "life." We're going to take a three-dimensional look at how the Bible describes the corrupt heart in order to see what we can discover about it.

A Hard Heart

Starting with the first dimension, let's look at what the Bible calls the hardhearted community and see what it has to offer us in our daily lives. Just the sound of "hard heart" makes it seem as if it will have nothing pleasant for us to look at. As a matter of fact, when we leave this hardhearted community, I'm quite sure we will be ready to move on to something more appealing.

Every time you watch the news or pick up a newspaper, you will find articles that depict a hardhearted person. Such a person is defined as someone who is pitiless, callous, cruel, and without feeling. Many of the acts some people commit toward other human beings are unbelievable. Those horrific acts certainly fit the definition of a hardhearted person.

A person who has a hardened heart in his or her natural state is easy to understand — that is, without Christ Jesus in his or her life. However, imagining Christians coming to a point in their lives where they have hardened their hearts is more difficult. Keep in mind that the Bible warns of this very possibility. Our focus in this section of the book is on believers who have hardened their hearts.

I cannot think of a more desolate, despicable, or debasing condition to be in than to have developed a hardened heart. If we should be found in such a condition, I pray that we would deeply consider softening our hearts. Let's take a glance at the dynamics of how a hard heart is conceived and developed in a person's life.

The Source of a Hard Heart

First, clearly God can harden a person's heart. Interestingly, the ten plagues came on Pharaoh and the people of Egypt because Pharaoh had a hardened heart. However, this fact shouldn't come as a surprise. In 1 Kings 8:38, Solomon wrote of every person knowing the plague of his or her own heart. A person's heart in its natural state is plagued, unhealthy, and diseased with sin. The Bible offers several examples of men with hardened hearts; we should learn from them and not let our own hearts be hardened. We should never lose sight of the fact that God works in the hearts of human beings. He can administer hardness if He chooses and administer mercy as He pleases. Never underestimate God's power; He can carry out whatever He wants in the lives of men.

And the Lord said unto Moses, when thou goest to return into Egypt, see that thou do all these wonders before Pharaoh, which I have put in thine hand: but I will harden his heart, that he shall not let the people go.
—*Exod. 4:21 (emphasis added)*

He hath blinded their eyes, and hardened their heart; *that they shouldn't see with their eyes, nor understand with their heart, and be converted, and I should heal them.*
—*John 12:40 (emphasis added)*

Second, clearly people can harden their own hearts. The writer of the Book of Hebrews used Scripture from Psalm 95 to state his case. The writer addressed God's people and warned them to be careful: if they had heard God's word, they shouldn't harden their hearts as their forefathers had done in the past. I've personally stood at the bedside of a few hardhearted people as their final days were winding down. I can assure you that the peace that had escaped them while they were living also escaped them while they were dying.

I want to point out, however, that although we may say we will never harden our hearts, we should remember that the situations the disciples found themselves in, which caused them to harden their own hearts, didn't seem that severe to me. Therefore we should understand that we must be watchful so that in drastic situations in which we may find ourselves, we won't harden our hearts. We can look at the examples of people who actually walked with Jesus and witnessed His miraculous power, yet they still had their hearts hardened. How much easier could it be for any of us who walk with the Lord by faith and not by sight to harden our hearts in a dire situation?

> Therefore, as the Holy Spirit says, "Today, if you hear his voice, *do not harden your hearts* as in the rebellion, on the day of testing in the wilderness, where your fathers put me to the test and saw my works for forty years. Therefore I was provoked with that generation, and said, 'They always go astray in their heart, they have not known my ways.' As I swore in my wrath, 'They shall not enter my rest.'" Take care, brothers, lest there be in any of you an evil, unbelieving heart, leading you to fall away from the living God. But exhort one another every day, as long as it is called "today," that none of you may be *hardened* by the deceitfulness of sin. For we have come to share in Christ, if indeed we hold our

original confidence firm to the end. As it is said, "Today, if you hear his voice, *do not harden your hearts* as in the rebellion." (Heb. 3:7–15 ESV, emphasis added)

For they did not understand about the loaves, but their *hearts were hardened*. (Mark 6:52, ESV emphasis added)

The Image of a Hardened Heart

And I will give them one heart, and I will put a new spirit within you; and I will take the stony *heart out of their flesh, and will give them an heart of flesh.*
—*Ezek. 11:19 (emphasis added)*

A hard heart has the image of a stone that has no pores. Pores allow your heart to receive love and affection from God and other people. For that matter you cannot give love and affection to other people if you aren't receiving them from God.

Pick up a rock and take a good look at it. What do you see? You will see the same thing you would see if you could pick up a heart of stone and look at it.

A rock is hard, and it's hard to the very core. Therefore no impression can be placed on it; nothing can penetrate the hardness of the rock, so it rejects anything that tries to leave its mark on it. A hard heart isn't soft enough to receive a pattern or mark that God or any person might try to make on it. It rejects all efforts directed to it through ministry or message.

A rock is cold and projects no warmth to the person who clutches it in his or her hand. A hardhearted person is cold and lacks the ability and qualities to produce a warm relationship with anyone.

A rock is dead and has no feeling. You could do anything you desire to that rock, and it would never respond. The same could be said about a person with a hard heart, for it is callous and incapable of feeling. A hard heart is dull and insensitive to God and people.

The Effects of a Hard Heart

Having eyes, see ye not? and have ears, hear ye not? and do ye not remember?
—Mark 8:18 ASV

In the Scripture quoted above, we see how dull our senses become due to the effects of a hard heart. Our perception will be hindered; we won't clearly see the teachings of the word of God. We may be able to see physically with twenty-twenty vision, but we'll be blind to the spiritual things of God. Having eyes, we see not. Our hearing will be muted to the message of God as the Spirit of God teaches us truths of the Bible. To us God will be much like the cell-phone advertisement on television; the man holds a cell phone, but a huge building blocks him. In the commercial he says, "Can you hear me now?"

God may be talking to us, but we will be unable to hear Him. With a hard heart, there will be no reception on our end of the line when God speaks to us. Our spiritual brain cells will become dead. We no longer will be able to remember the marvelous things God has done in our lives. Seemingly these memories have been erased from our minds.

A hardened heart in the life of a Christian isn't always a matter of falling away from God. In fact it can happen in the midst of church activity. Everyone has likely known someone in church who was faithful to services, gave financially, and may have even held a particular office — but he or she was one of the most wicked people we've ever met. In the Bible there is an example of a two-pronged source of hard hearts in the story of the prodigal son. In the story the heart of the prodigal son was hardened due to his selfishness. The heart of his older brother was hardened because of his self-righteousness.

A Wicked Heart

But what comes out of the mouth proceeds from the heart, and this defiles a person. For out of the heart come evil thoughts, murder, adultery, sexual immorality, theft, false witness, slander. These are what defile a person. But to eat with unwashed hands does not defile anyone.
—Matt. 15:18–20 ESV

Evil is the real problem in the hearts and minds of men. It is not a problem of physics but ethics. It is easier to denature plutonium than to denature the evil spirit of man.
—Albert Einstein

The second dimension we will look at is what the Bible calls a wicked-hearted community. Having departed from the hardhearted community, we have traveled only a short distance and arrived at the wicked-hearted community. These communities are close in distance because a hard heart begins the process of developing a wicked heart. In other words those in the hardhearted community decided to establish a suburb a short distance down the highway, and they called it the "wicked-heart community."

No one wakes up one morning and decides he or she is going to become a wicked person. Developing a wicked heart is a deceitful process that takes place over a period of time. Wickedness slowly but surely overcomes us in a way that lulls us to sleep so we aren't aware of the process until it overtakes us, and then we have become wicked people.

The process is much like putting a frog in a pan of water and gradually heating that water until it's at boiling point. The frog becomes accustomed to the heating water and fails to recognize the danger it's in. Moreover if you were to just drop a frog into boiling water, it would hop out immediately. Wickedness slowly develops in our lives, and we fail to recognize its danger until it's too late.

We're going to take a look at how wicked hearts develop, how they affect us, and what God sees when looking at a wicked heart. Not only that, but we're also going to see how a wicked heart affects God.

It Delivers No Value

The heart of the wicked is little worth.
—Prov. 10:20b

As you can see, the Bible says a wicked heart dispenses absolutely no value. The natural thinking of a wicked person is that his or her heart is valuable; therefore his or her way of life is valuable. Later we will see how pride enters into the mind-set of a wicked person. Arrogance becomes the persona of a wicked person.

In our culture we have become experts at knowing the price of an item without knowing anything about its value. The Bible speaks of counting the cost of our spiritual lives, but it is more concerned about the value of our spiritual lives. A wicked heart is worth nothing, is good for nothing, and provides no return on its investment. It would be wise to take a moment to calculate the value of our own hearts.

It Imagines Evil Deeds

> *And God saw that the wickedness of man was great in the earth, and that every imagination of the thoughts of his heart was only evil continually.*
> —Gen. 6:5

The kinds of images we allow to develop in our minds are very important. The mind is never in a vacuum, so there will be images in it. The examples in Scripture we find were evil imaginations that were continually thinking of other evil deeds to accomplish. Scripture makes it clear that these evil imaginations were constant and that these people made certain to carry out those evil deeds. Not one imagination was left unturned, for the Bible says every imagination was of an evil heart. The people certainly didn't walk in the way of God, for they wouldn't hearken unto Him.

It Defiles a Person

> *Do you not see that whatever goes into the mouth passes into the stomach and is expelled? But what comes out of the mouth proceeds from the heart, and this defiles a person. For out of the heart come evil thoughts, murder, adultery, sexual immorality, theft, false witness, slander. These are what defile a person. But to eat with unwashed hands does not defile anyone.*
> —Matt. 15:17–20 ESV

An evil thought is the fountain that gushes forth into an evil act. The text above lists the various sinful actions that can be produced. Though we try very hard to suppress these immoral thoughts and actions, they still pollute and defile us. Pollution in our hearts is the true source of the sinful deeds listed above. As you can see, an array of evil vices is produced from the deep, inward pollution of a wicked heart. A defiled person is one who is corrupt in terms of morals, principles, and character.

It Produces Pride

The wicked in his pride doth persecute the poor: let them be taken in the devices that they have imagined. For the wicked boasteth of his heart's desire, and blesseth the covetous, whom the Lord abhorreth.
—*Ps. 10:2–3*

The psalmist described the attitude of this pride-driven person. The following list describes the attitude of a wicked heart. The attitudes are very evident and cannot be concealed. Conceit is evident in a wicked person's heart. An evil person is obsessed with himself or herself and boasts of his or her heart's desires. A disregard of God works in his or her heart or mind. This person won't seek God, and God isn't in his or her thoughts. Obstinacy is apparent in his or her way of living.

This person declares that God isn't going to move him or her and that nothing awful is going to happen to him or her. Craftiness is the wicked person's way of seeking and destroying his or her enemies. He or she lurks in hidden places of the city and waits secretly like a lion to pounce on the poor. An evil heart is always on the prowl. Irrationality has overtaken his or her heart.

These people think in their hearts that God has forgotten about them or that God won't see what they are thinking or doing. They don't believe God knows about them or cares; therefore God won't bring them to justice.

It Is Detested by God

> *These six things doth the LORD hate: yea, seven are an abomination unto him: A proud look, a lying tongue, and hands that shed innocent blood. An heart that devises wicked imaginations, feet that be swift in running to mischief, a false witness that speaks lies, and he that soweth discord among brethren.*
> *—Prov. 6:16-19*

Hearing the word *hate* used in respect to a God of love is difficult for us. However, it's comforting to know that the things listed in the above Scripture — and not the people who do these things — are what God hates,. We've all likely heard many times that God hates the sin but loves the sinner. You will notice that in the middle of this Scripture, the writer declares that God hates a wicked heart that devises wicked imaginations.

Now we have ventured into almost every section of this community. I don't know about you, but there's nothing I find in this community that would make me want to take up residence there. I think it's time for us to exit the wicked-hearted community and drive further down the road in the journey of the heart. Surely there is a heart community where we can live that would be more pleasing to our Savior.

A Deceitful Heart

The heart is deceitful above all things, and desperately wicked: who can know it?
—Jer. 17:9

The third dimension we will look at is what the Bible calls a deceitful-heart community. We now find ourselves in a new location as we make our eighteen-inch journey from the head to the heart. We have left behind the communities of hardhearted and wicked-hearted people and have traveled down the road to deceitful-hearted people.

Believe me, the journey gets better and the scenery more beautiful the further we travel on our spiritual highway. Don't give up on this journey yet; I promise you that if you are serious about your spiritual journey, it has the possibility of taking you to a beautiful, joyful, and peaceful community where you can reside.

Let me ask you a question. Do you know your heart? Most of us would no doubt say yes, believing we have a pretty good knowledge of who we are. Well, let me ask you another question. Would you be willing to have your heart exposed on television for the entire world to see? It seems reasonable that we should know our own hearts and their true character, because we're the ones who have access to them.

Can you believe that God would present even the possibility of our not knowing who we are? After all, our culture offers all the scientific and medical expertise, technological advancement, and intellectual superiority known to humankind to help us know everything about our hearts. I'm going to ask the next question in a different way. If you were standing face-to-face with God, and He said, "You cannot know your heart," what would you say to Him? Would you argue with Him about His statement?

When we arrive in an area that is unfamiliar, it's always helpful to stop and pick up some information about the community. Let's stop in the visitors' center to see what this community has to offer us for life. Let's see what the information packet has to say about a deceitful heart and, more important, about what God has to say about our hearts.

How Could It Be That We Cannot Know Our Own Hearts?

I would surmise that the reason we don't have the ability to know our own hearts is that we have an inherent ability within us for self-praise and worship. In fact we idolize ourselves to the point that we begin to believe we're much better than we really are. This is why the apostle Paul warned us in Romans 12:3, "For I say, through the grace given unto me, to every man that is among you, not to think of himself more highly than he ought to think; but to think soberly, according as God hath dealt to every man the measure of faith"

We have the tendency to see the deceitfulness in the hearts of those around us but to never acknowledge our own deceitful hearts. When we find ourselves in conflict with our relationships — whether they are in our family, church, or social setting — we usually slant our opinion about the reason for the conflict. We do this to the point that it will make us look good, and we can place the blame on the other person. Though we may try to deceive another person, in actuality we're deceiving ourselves. Why is this so? It's because of our attitude of self-importance, which blinds us from seeing our deceitful hearts.

Here we are, intelligent beings, but God says we're ignorant of our true character. In a deceitful way, we try to justify our own behavior before others and God. This deceitfulness shows up in various ways in our lives. The two ways that stand out the most are found in the thoughts and intents of our hearts. That is why the writer of Hebrews 4:12 reminds us that even though we might not discern the deceitfulness of our hearts, we can be assured that the word of God is a discerner of the thoughts and intents of our hearts. That principle is rooted deeply in our lives, to the very core of our being. From out of the heart, our conduct proceeds; therefore our conduct has the ability to be deceitful.

The root word for *deceit* actually speaks of the arrogance and self-pride that so often blind us to the condition of our hearts. Jacob, the one the Bible calls the supplanter, is a prime illustration of what the word *deceit* actually means. We're going to follow the trail of the Hebrew word for *deceit*.

The Hebrew word for *deceitful* is found in Jeremiah 17:9: "The heart is deceitful above all things, and desperately wicked; who can know it?" The word is *aqob*, which was originally defined as "a hill, a knoll, or a swelling up."[3] This definition leads us to the reason we cannot know our hearts. As I mentioned earlier, this is due to pride and our own self-indulgent thinking that we're greater than we actually are. In other words our egos swell up beyond the boundaries of rational thinking.

Genesis 25:26 describes Jacob as his hand took hold of Esau's heel — *heel* meaning "a protuberance or the rear of an army,"[4] which comes from the Hebrew word *aqeb*. Jacob is named in this same verse. His name comes from the Hebrew word *ya-aqob*, which means "a heel catcher."[5]

---

3 *Brown-Driver-Briggs Hebrew and English Lexicon;* Francis Brown, Samuel Rolles Driver, Charles A. Briggs; Snowball Publishing; 2010
4 Ibid.
5 Ibid.

We find Jacob's deceitfulness as he came before his father, Isaac, and pretended to be Esau. Jacob tricked his father into passing his blessing on to him, which rightfully belonged to his brother Esau. In this verse Esau said about Jacob: "Is not he rightly named Jacob? for he hath supplanted me these two times: he took away my birthright; and, behold, now he hath taken away my blessing" (Gen. 27:36). In this verse the word *supplanted* comes from the Hebrew word *aqab*, which means "a heel catcher, a knoll, a swelling up."[6]

What Can We Know about What We Cannot Know?

What we know is that we cannot know our own hearts. God is extremely clear about that statement. The reason we cannot know our own hearts is summarized in the definition of the word *deceitful*. The words used to describe *deceitful* are numerous. The word *deceive* can be described as giving a bogus impression of oneself, cheating to get one's way, hoodwinking someone, or leading someone off course from his or her true path. As I mentioned before, these same words are found in the life and actions of Jacob, the supplanter.

It's no wonder we so often ask ourselves why we behaved a certain way, why we said what we just said, or why we treated people the way we did. We know in our hearts that this behavior isn't who we are, yet we do these things. When an evil thought runs through our minds, we wonder where the thought came from. Often people find themselves involved in a sin they never thought they would succumb to.

These things happen because we don't know ourselves. The image of our hearts has become somewhat distorted.

---

6 Ibid.

The Holy Potholes of Christianity

I remember going to the Kansas State Fair as a child. Those in charge always had a walk-through truck trailer filled with a fun house with curved mirrors. The mirrors distorted our height and girth to the point that we were unrecognizable. I remember the fun I had as a kid as I walked through the rows of crazy mirrors. They made me look skinny, heavy, short, tall, ugly, and sometimes handsome. In other words the mirrors were deceitful; the images portrayed weren't really what I looked like.

Our hearts are much like these curved mirrors. We look at ourselves and say, "Wait a minute. That isn't who I am." When we begin to think of ourselves more highly than we ought, this misperception becomes a danger point for the believer. When people arrive at a point in their Christian lives where they think they have become extremely pious, they are walking on dangerous ground.

Let me say this: your heart is deceiving you. It distorts your spiritual condition. That is the reason why we find ourselves justifying our own behavior while criticizing the behavior of our fellow believers. Our egos won't allow us to be transparent; therefore our relationships, mentioned previously, become superficial, confrontational, and head-to-head relationships. From out of hearts come the issues of life.

I suppose that as we leave this deceitful-heart community, there is one thing we *do* know: our hearts are deceitful, and we cannot know them. As our hearts change, let's move on to the outskirts of our next heart community and see what it has in store for us. You may be confused in this next community. Nothing is marked very well, and even if you have a GPS, you may find yourself wandering around, trying to find your location.

Chapter 6

A Confused Heart

Having left the first leg of our heart journey, called the "corrupt heart," we now begin the second part, which is called the "confused heart." To be honest with you, while I was in this state of a confused heart, it was a very dark hour for me, and I still needed the headlights to maneuver through this community. I suppose some of the characteristics of the corrupt heart were still very evident in my life at this point in the journey.

On this leg of our excursion, we will examine three conditions of the heart that I believe cause confusion in our lives; these three conditions rise above the conditions of the corrupt heart. Nevertheless if we allow them to continue, they will stymie our spiritual growth and complicate the various levels of our relationships. They take us a step closer to our quest of finding a pure, clean heart to live by. But we're still miles away from attaining that clean, transparent, tranquil, and peaceful heart.

A confused state is one in which we find ourselves puzzled and perplexed. Again it is a state in which we cannot see things clearly. The pain and emotional state of our hearts cloud the inward eyes we look through. We see much like one would see when he or she develops a cataract. Let me illustrate this confused and somewhat-blurred spiritual sight with an example of a physical eye affected by a specific disease.

My wife — along with two of our three sons — had a partial cornea transplant in both eyes due to an eye disease called Fuchs' dystrophy. This disease causes the eyesight to become blurred, and the sensation has been described as looking through sheer curtains or a steamed-over shower door. With this disease my wife could look at a person, but his or her features weren't clear; the person looked like a silhouette. Another symptom of Fuchs' dystrophy is the fading of colors, which becomes unnoticeable after the cornea transplant. After the surgery there comes that "wow moment" when colors are bright and clear once more.

When hitting a golf ball, our youngest son could never see the ball once it was in flight. Someone would have to watch the flight and let him know its direction and how far the ball had traveled. When playing golf with my son, I saw how confused, puzzled, and perplexed he was simply because he couldn't see clearly. He once told me that in a way he had learned to be deceitful by letting people think he could see what he actually couldn't.

Just as Fuchs' dystrophy limited the eyesight of my wife and two sons, the three areas of a confused heart can cause the same effects in our spiritual lives. Just as a hard heart, wicked heart, and deceitful heart cause great damage in our various relationships, a wounded heart, troubled heart, and grieving heart will cause damage in much the same way. However, the damage will possibly be on a lesser level than the damage of the previous heart conditions.

We see aspects of the following three heart conditions in the lives of many people today. We often see the attitudes and actions of these conditions in marriages, family lives, workplaces, and churches. There are several reasons someone can experience such a heart condition. Someone who hurt us or a natural, unpleasant situation that passed through our lives can leave that type of pain in our hearts. Let's look at some of life's situations that produce the pain we find in these three areas.

A Wounded Heart

For I am poor and needy, and my heart is wounded within me.
—Ps. 109:22

The spirit of a man will sustain his infirmity, but a wounded spirit who can bear?
—Prov. 18:14

The first negative condition of a confused heart is what the Bible calls a "wounded heart." I want you to think about what it's like to have a physical wound. Think about what caused the wound in the first place; then think about the pain it produced. Next you waited for a scab to form over the wound so it could heal completely, and finally a scar was left behind as a reminder.

This same process takes place when we are wounded in our spiritual hearts, spirits, or emotions. First comes the wound, then the pain and the scab. Later the scar is a reminder of the past. Just as we desire a physical wound to heal, we should desire a spiritual and emotional wound to heal rather than allow it to fester and cause confusion in the future.

Ratsa, the Hebrew word for *wound*, simply means "to bore or pierce."[7] Imagine the piercing of a sword wounding a heart. We find an image or description of this type of nasty, painful wound when Simeon blessed Joseph and Mary. "And Simeon blessed

---
7 *Strong's Concordance,* http://biblehub.com/hebrew/7527.htm

them, and said unto Mary his mother, Behold, this child is set for the fall and rising again of many in Israel; and for a sign which shall be spoken against; Yea, a sword shall *pierce* through thy own soul also, that the thought of many hearts may be revealed" (Luke 2:34–35, emphasis added).

The following section lists some of the ways a person or some unpleasant situation in our lives can wound us emotionally.

Personal Attacks

Wounds from a personal attack often come our way as the result of an abusive person attacking us. Cutting words are used as the weapon of verbal abuse. People who verbally abuse others were often verbally abused as children. Their abusive behavior may have begun when they were children when a parent constantly targeted them, cutting into their psyche. Verbal abuse is often carried into the child's teenage years and even into adulthood if it isn't dealt with in a positive, healing way. This abuse may happen in many different settings and surroundings, such as verbal abuse targeted at a spouse through cutting words. An employee might work with a supervisor who is verbally abusive. Of course there are always people in the church setting who are more than ready to use their tongues to abuse other believers by cutting them down with their words.

Another form of abuse is physical abuse. Anyone who has been the recipient of physical abuse knows how demeaning it is and will probably carry the scars of such behavior for many years, possibly even for the rest of his or her life, if it isn't dealt with. Every occasion of the hand being used to hit someone creates another piercing of the heart, another wound, another scab, another scar.

Yet another form of abuse is sexual abuse, which is probably the most diabolical weapon anyone could use against another person to pierce his or her heart with pain. The wounds are deep and heal slowly. The scars are often seen for many years. Only by the grace of God can these wounds heal.

These personal attacks usually cause a tremendous amount of confusion in our lives — to the extent that we're unable to clearly see our own personal being or to understand who we truly are and how life works out in daily living. On top of not being able to see ourselves clearly, we're unable to get a clear glimpse of God, how He works in our lives, and how He can enable us to move forward in our lives and leave the pain behind.

Personal Rejection

Rejection is also a type of tool or weapon that can pierce the heart of an individual. Rejection can wound a heart, often causing deep depression. I recall situations when I felt rejected and hurt as a child. In grade school I was usually the last person selected when the baseball-team captains chose players. In high school the group of popular teens never accepted or included me.

In your life maybe a girlfriend or boyfriend broke up with you, and you felt rejected and deeply wounded. Maybe you've experienced something more painful than a breakup. Maybe you've gone through a divorce, and your spouse ordered you out of the house, demanding that you sign divorce papers. Possibly someone else got the job your heart was set on, and you felt your supervisor's rejection.

One of the loneliest places you can find yourself is in a church worship service surrounded by thousands of people but feeling that no one cares about you. There are countless ways you can feel rejected and many ways in which you've probably already experienced rejection. Once again the heart becomes confused. As a Christian I know you shouldn't be confused, but no matter who you are, this event will surely happen.

A wounded heart produces confusion and causes us to see through the eyes of that wound, distorting our spiritual vision. When you have a physical wound, touching it can be extremely painful. Having a wounded heart is one reason many people become isolated and won't allow others to get too close to them. This response arises from a fear of the pain they might feel if another person touches them in the sore spot of their painful wound.

A Troubled Heart

Let not your heart be troubled: ye believe in God, believe also in me.
—John 14:1

The second negative condition of a confused heart is a troubled heart. I believe everyone has a desire to experience peace in his or her heart, and when I speak of peace, I mean the peace of God that surpasses all understanding. God definitely wants us to experience His peace, which is so much different from the peace that the world offers and that so many people pursue. This doesn't mean everyone will experience peace at all times, but we should move in that direction continually.

Our Scripture speaks of a troubled heart. The word *troubled* simply means a heart that is anxious, upset, or agitated. Again a troubled heart produces a confused heart. I would like to point out a few things the Bible mentions that will cause a troubled heart.

A Confused Heart

The disciples had a sense of insecurity because they'd been in a close relationship with Jesus and His ministry; they knew Jesus was going to leave them soon, and their hearts were troubled. They were insecure in their own ability to carry on in their spiritual lives and in the ministry He had begun. Our insecurity comes when we trust in our own abilities, which often causes us to experience a troubled heart.

The disciples had a sense of fear because Jesus was going to return and receive them unto Himself. His return was something very difficult for them to comprehend and assimilate; therefore their hearts were troubled and confused because of their fear of their future. Most of us at some point in our lives have experienced a troubled heart, because we're scared of what the future holds for us.

The disciples had a sense of doubt, which happened as the result of their lack of understanding. In John 14:5, Thomas said, "Lord, we know not whither thou goest." Since they didn't know where Jesus was going, they had doubt; and that doubt produced troubled hearts, and troubled hearts produced confusion. Living by faith isn't an easy principle to practice. Due to our lack of understanding, we begin to doubt what Christ is able to do in our lives, and this doubt leads to a troubled heart and ultimately confusion.

A troubled heart is one that lacks the peace of God. In the Bible, Jesus tell us not to allow a troubled heart into our lives. In other words we shouldn't let our hearts be troubled.

Living life with a troubled heart will produce anxiety; and anxiety will produce confusion, and anxious moments will spill over into all our relationships, because we cannot see the issues of life clearly.

A Grieving Heart

Thus my heart was grieved, and I was pricked in my reins.
—Ps. 73:21

Wherefore the king said unto me, why is thy countenance sad, seeing thou art not sick? This is nothing else but sorrow of heart. Then I was very sore afraid.
—Neh. 2:2

The third negative condition of a confused heart is a grieving heart. It's a heart that is filled with sorrow, anguish, and suffering. The loss of something very precious to us typically produces this heart, causing us to grieve that loss.

In my many years of being a pastor, I have found that when people experience the death of a loved one, they go through a painful grieving stage in dealing with that loss. At first they find themselves in a state of confusion. They cannot understand why the death had to happen or why God took their loved one so soon. Their state of confusion, due to the death of their loved one, affects their personal behavior and attitude and can often lead them to have faulty or damaged relationships.

Sometimes parents lose a child to death. This event would be unimaginably painful and hard to overcome, but it is a crucial time for a husband and wife to come together and not allow the confusion of a grieving heart to separate them. Many couples have dealt with the tragic loss of a child, but instead of coming together in their grief, they allowed that grief to overtake them and consequently end their marriage forever in divorce. These couples were in a state of confusion.

Though a loss typically produces grief, there are many other situations we may encounter that may cause us to grieve as well. Parents often grieve when they see a decline in the academic status, morals, or lifestyle of their children. Parents also go through a grieving phase when their relationships with their children decline, and they become estranged from their children. There certainly should be a sense of grieving if we find ourselves falling into degradation or a state of deep sin. There's no doubt we grieve when we find ourselves or someone we love in a state of moral decline. Moral decline is due to the presence of sin in our lives and the shame we experience due to that sin. This leads to the loss of moral standing in our relationships.

A grieving heart will shed a lot of tears and produce a state of confusion. A grieving heart looks through the eyes of despair. These eyes cannot see clearly and may hinder our very close relationships.

When we find ourselves in the state of a confused heart, we will continue to communicate in our various relationships with the head-to-head style, which creates a great deal of strife and conflict with people we love very much.

Why is this so? Because when we live with a wounded, troubled, or grieving heart, our inward eyes cannot see clearly. Actually we can become so confused that we want to opt out of many of our relationships. To be honest with you, in my own case, I was ready to quit the ministry and toss the Christian life overboard, because at the time it didn't seem to be working for me. Why did I think it wasn't working? I believe the fact that I couldn't see clearly caused this problem. Though I never contemplated a separation or divorce from my dear wife, I certainly shut her out of my life for a complete year while I lived in deep depression because I couldn't see clearly.

The positive side of having a confused heart is the fact that we can find healing for a wounded, troubled, and grieving heart. Once we find that healing, battle scars may remain, but at least we can move on to the next leg of our journey. The reason we can move on in our spiritual journey at this point is that when healing comes, it begins to restore our eyesight to its original state.

The next level is what I call a curious heart. A curious heart is one that is always questioning, probing, and prying as to how to find the peace of God and how to arrive at a pure heart.

However, before we start the engine, put it in gear, and pop the clutch of life to start this leg of the journey, let me remind you of this: *out of the heart come the issues of life.* The topics discussed in the next chapter help us answer the question "Does Christianity work?"

Chapter 7
A Curious Heart

I call to remembrance my song in the night: I commune with mine own heart: and my spirit made diligent search.
—Ps. 77:6

The heart of him that hath understanding seeketh knowledge: but the mouth of fools feedeth on foolishness.
—Prov. 15:14

    Finding our way through the maze of our spiritual lives will undoubtedly require us to have a spiritual GPS to steer us in the direction we need to be traveling on the map of our lives — the map God has already laid out for us. Yogi Berra, the great catcher for the New York Yankees, once said, "When you come to a fork in the road, take it."

    The curious stage of our journey can actually be a fork in the road for a believer. When we come to that fork, we will take it one way or the other. It is here that we will take either the fork that will lead us right back to where we came from, away from God, or the fork that will lead us closer to Him. One way leads toward a life filled with conflict and the pain that comes with that conflict. This, in turn, produces broken and shattered relationships. The other way will enable us to find peace and joy in our Christian lives and enjoy the relationships we've established.

    It is at this point in our journey that we can begin to find the answers to the question "Does Christianity work?" When we become curious enough about our spiritual lives, God, and our relationships with Him, we begin to sense that the answer to that question is yes. Christianity *does* work. We find that Christianity isn't — and never has been — the problem in our lives; rather we begin to realize that our problems are in the heart. From out of the heart come the issues of life.

We become tired of living in the cesspool of a corrupt heart and in the anguish of a confused heart. We grow tired of being discouraged and depressed because every relationship we've had has been on a head-to-head basis. We become so tired that we come to a pivotal point in our spiritual life journey where we finally get on the road of a curious heart. This road will actually take us to a place that is pleasant and enjoyable, and our spiritual lives begin to move in a new and more positive direction.

The definition of *curious* is "to arouse attention, to be inquisitive, or to have a new interest."[8] Curiosity is the catalyst that nudges us to a place where we can see things more clearly, and it moves us into the action of correcting the direction we're going in our spiritual lives. We're at the point where Christianity becomes clearer and the features more definable. Curiosity is an inner desire to learn and know the word of God and to learn how to apply the word of God to our lives.

You may wonder what spiritual curiosity actually is and what triggers it in our lives. Let me give you two examples of spiritual curiosity from the life of the apostle Paul. The first example is when Paul stated very strongly, "That I may know him" (Phil. 3:10). Paul wasn't talking about a greater intellectual knowledge of God; rather he was curious about having an experiential knowledge of God, knowing that it would take him into a deeper

---

8 *Webster's New World College Dictionary,* 4th edition, Wiley Publishing

relationship with the Lord Jesus Christ. He knew this would mean having an intimate relationship with Jesus Christ.

The second example is when Paul stated, "Brethren, I count not myself to have apprehended: but this one thing I do, forgetting those things which are behind, and reaching forth unto those things which are before, I press toward the mark for the prize of the high calling of God in Christ Jesus" (Phil. 3:13-14). Paul was so curious and wanted to know God so badly that this drive inspired him to set out on a pursuit of God, taking him in a new direction. Rather than looking back on his life journey and its pain, he began to look forward to his life's journey and its gain. Spiritual curiosity is having a desire to learn and know more about God and your relationship with Christ, which moves you forward in your spiritual life.

That which triggers curiosity can be found through the utterance of the psalmist Asaph. "I cried unto God with my voice, even unto God with my voice; and he gave ear unto me. In the day of my trouble I sought the Lord: my sore ran in the night, and ceased not: my soul refused to be comforted. I remembered God, and was troubled: I complained, and my spirit was overwhelmed. Selah" (Ps. 77:1-3). In the first verse, the psalmist speaks of his crying unto God, which his trouble, described in verse two, prompted. He was troubled, downcast, depressed — putting together his song in the night. It was in those moments that he became curious and communed with his heart while his spirit made a diligent search.

Two things are imperative at the juncture of a curious heart. It is at this point that we must look deeply into our hearts to face reality and desire honesty and authenticity within ourselves. We're more apt, however, to look deeply into the heart of another person rather than into our own hearts. This journey isn't about the other person; it's about us. Here we must ask tough questions about our own hearts and our own inner person.

If you aren't willing to take the following steps, your heart will likely remain in its present condition. You will continue to have head-to-head, confrontational relationships and find that they will fail. You will never find peace and tranquility in life. You will also never experience the heart-to-heart relationships God intended for you to have with Him and the people in the circle of your relationships.

Search Your Heart

Ask the Tough Questions

> *As a deer longs for flowing streams, so my soul longs for you, O God. My soul thirsts for God, for the living God. When may I come to see God's face? My tears are my food day and night. People ask me all day long, "Where is your God?" I will remember these things as I pour out my soul: how I used to walk with the crowd and lead it in a procession to God's house. I sang songs of joy and thanksgiving while crowds of people celebrated a festival. Why are you discouraged, my soul? Why are you so restless? Put your hope in God, because I will still praise him. He is my savior and my God. My soul is discouraged. That is why I will remember you in the land of Jordan, on the peaks of Hermon, on Mount Mizar.*
> —Ps. 42:1–6 GW

In this Scripture the psalmist once again cried out to God and did some in-depth soul-searching. He personally examined the condition of his heart. He shared with us that he knew and understood that something wasn't right with him and his relationship with his heavenly Father. He was extremely curious; notice his passion for God in verse one, in which he declared that his heart panted after God. He later went on to say that his heart thirsted for God.

In verse four he exposed the anguish of his heart by saying, "I pour out my soul in me." Then the psalmist asked himself a very tough question: "Why are you cast down, O my soul, and why are you in turmoil with me?" In other words something was awry in his life, and it was tormenting him. He asked, "Why am I living a life of deep depression?" I have been there; I guess the question to ask is "Have you experienced this kind of life?"

His curiosity caused him to ask difficult questions. Recall our previous text, when the psalmist said, "I commune with mine own heart: and my spirit made diligent search" (Ps. 77:6b).

The first step to move from head-to-head, worldly behavior to heart-to-heart Christian behavior is to communicate with and search your heart; ask yourself the tough questions. Christians who have a desire to make a successful Christian journey — one that is faithful, full, and fruitful — will eventually ask tough questions about their hearts. When you're curious about God and your relationship with Him, you will be curious enough to ask tough questions.

Allow God to Search Your Heart

Accept the Tough Answers

Once we've searched our hearts and asked ourselves the tough questions, the next step is to be willing to ask God to search our hearts and allow us to receive the tough answers. This is the very thing David did when he asked God to search his heart. "Search me, O God, and know my heart: try me, and know my thoughts: And see if there be any wicked way in me, and lead me in the way everlasting" (Ps. 139:23-24).

Jeremiah declared the Lord's intention for participating in this process when he wrote, "I the Lord search the heart, I try the reins, even to give every man according to his ways, and according to the fruit of his doings" (Jer. 17:10)

In our culture it's a common practice to examine the lives of our mates, our children, our coworkers, or our fellow church members rather than our own lives. We tend to look at the splinter in our brother's eye but fail to notice the plank in our own. This is why our lives never change for the better and why we go on for years with the same old, cold heart. We're willing to live with the same heartache. We seem satisfied to live with the same empty heart and the same troubled, grieving, wounded heart. This is the very reason life becomes the pits to many people in our Christian culture today. This is why many people throw their hands up and exclaim, "If this is what Christianity is all about, then count me out, for I want nothing to do with its claim."

This is the fork in the road I came to in 1983 when I was contemplating and considering giving up on Christianity. When I was a young boy, I came to know Christ as my Lord and Savior, and I had the advantage of attending a little country church where I was grounded in the doctrines of the Bible. I had wonderful parents who set before me a great example of how to live my life. I married an extraordinary woman, whom I love dearly, and we have three children who are a blessing to us, as are their families.

I entered full-time ministry as a pastor when I was thirty years old. I was married and had three small boys. I had the privilege of founding a Baptist church in 1971 and pastoring for twelve years in Kansas and in the Washington, DC, area. Despite all of these blessings, I found that my spiritual life tank was on empty. In my heart there was the absence of the peace and joy I knew were available to me. Part of the reason I experienced this emptiness was because I had grown up in a church that had done a great job teaching us how to die, but seldom was there a word on how to live.

During this time God allowed an ugly, painful situation to enter my life when a church member angrily bolted up during one of my sermons and yelled, "Why don't you just preach the truth?" That incident led our church through years of devastation. During this period of time, I found out that our first grandbaby was to be born with hydrocephalus, and the news nearly crushed our entire family.

Rodney was born with several disabilities and lived a short life of only three years. Those years became very precious for our family and me, and Rodney taught us so much about humility. When he was born, I received an anonymous card from someone in our church that said, "Isn't it a shame that a little baby has to suffer for the sins of its grandfather?" I felt as if someone had shot an arrow into my heart. At the time I wondered, *How can anyone be so wicked to make such a statement?* I thought, *If this is what Christianity produces, I'm not sure this is the road I want to travel any longer.*

The birth and death of our grandbaby, along with the hatred spewed out in the card, threw me into a deep depression for a complete year. It was during that dark year that I shut my dear wife out of my life. All she could do for me during that year was pray for me. I really didn't care whether I lived or died. What appeared obvious to me was that Christianity wasn't working for me; in fact it seemed as if it were actually working *against* me. I became so angry with God that He allowed these events to transpire in my life. I asked myself, *Really, does Christianity work?* I contemplated leaving the ministry and turning away from Christianity. I experienced an inner pain in my heart. It wasn't physical pain, but it was an inner, emotional pain, and it was with me twenty-four hours a day. There was a spiritual knot in my chest where my inner person was located. It was a big pothole I had encountered, and it came close to destroying my ministry and me.

It was at this juncture or fork in the road that God began to minister to me, much as he did to Elijah during his "juniper tree" experience. God's still, small voice constantly spoke to me throughout this ordeal. At this point God began to untie and release the spiritual knot I felt in my chest. It was amazing that the one I had angrily yelled at was now, in His quiet voice, talking to me about my future and what He had planned for me in the ministry for the rest of my life.

Wow, how excited I became that God had a plan for me. It was as if He were saying to me, "Buddy, you will find out how well Christianity works. Just hang on." God knew I was teachable. He took advantage of this teachable moment when He set up school in the classroom of my life and taught me how to live. He allowed me to be honest with myself and to realize there were changes I needed to make in my life and my attitude. I had to ask the tough questions, and I had to allow God to give me the tough answers. God's speaking to me in His still, quiet voice was so profound that it stirred up a consuming desire within me to seek and learn about God — and learn things about myself I had never known before, things only the Holy Spirit of God could teach me.

During this time I asked myself some tough questions: *What is wrong with my heart? Why is it so confused?* God's answers to my questions had to do with my ego. God revealed to me that I thought I was more important than I actually was. He revealed to me that I was playing the game of Christianity and hadn't allowed Him to be in control of my life. He pointed out to me that I was a fake and lacked real Christian authenticity. He exposed me to the fact that I was wearing a facade to cover up my emptiness.

This was a very humbling experience for me. However, as you will see in the chapters to follow, it was the greatest event that has ever happened to me to bring me to the point where I am today in my Christian life. It was then that God gave me the tough answers to the tough questions. It was then that my curious heart directed me to the next leg of my journey, which I call the "consuming heart."

I guess Yogi Berra was right. "When you come to the fork in the road, take it." Yes, you will take it, but it is vital to the advancement of your spiritual life that you take the correct fork. The journey is getting interesting and exciting at this point. How about we accelerate, take the correct fork in the road, and travel down the highway to the next leg of our journey to a consuming heart?

Chapter 8
A Consuming Heart

But they constrained him, saying, Abide with us; for it is toward evening, and the day is far spent. And he went in to tarry with them. And it came to pass, as he sat at meat with them, he took bread, and blessed it, and brake, and gave to them. And their eyes were opened, and they knew him; and he vanished out of their sight. And they said one to another, did not our heart burn within us, while he talked with us by the way, and while he opened to us the scriptures?
—Luke 24:29–32

When you are traveling, you will encounter many different kinds of scenery: landmarks, natural phenomena, snob hills, mansions, ghettos, shacks, farmland, and factories. Some filthy places you visit will disgust you. Some places will be very plain and lacking any exciting activity, so you will be bored with that area as you pass through. Some places will excite you due to various attractions found there. However, there will be times every so often when you will come upon something that will consume you and grab your attention.

In all my journeys, I have encountered many different levels of emotional experiences as I was passing through. These experiences were similar to the spiritual, emotional experiences I discussed in the previous chapters of this book.

For instance, when entering New York City, I found myself totally confused as to my location in the city. I was just as confused about how to find directions to the places I was looking for, such as the Statue of Liberty, the Empire State Building, Yankee Stadium, and other well-known landmarks.

On the other hand, when I was visiting and living in the Washington, DC, area, I experienced a totally different emotion. Here I experienced curiosity. My curiosity was aroused while I visited various museums, political institutions, Civil War sites, and many other historical sites surrounding the city. I remember being curious about my family heritage when visiting the National Archives. I tried to find information about my ancestors and searched for information about my family's journey from Germany to the United States in 1876. I remember how excited I was when I saw their names listed on the 1880 census, which had been recorded and stored on microfiche in the National Archives.

However, in various places during my travels, I've come upon some sites that stirred my heart so much that I became consumed with what was happening there. I remember sitting in a restaurant on the Canadian side of Niagara Falls and watching the energy being released as water flowed over the great falls. I was consumed with what I was witnessing. When I stood on the South Rim of the Grand Canyon, the beauty and vastness of the canyon left me awestruck. While sitting on a bench within a few feet of the Old Faithful geyser in Yellowstone National Park, I was reminded of how faithful and consistent that phenomenon truly is hour after hour. I became consumed with these three natural spectacles. My heart burned within me, and I was consumed with what I saw.

What we might experience as we travel around this great country of ours — or in another country on another continent — can be very similar to our experiences on our spiritual journey with the Lord Jesus Christ. I found this to be true in my relationship with God.

In previous chapters I spoke about those times when I was confused during my Christian journey. Yet there were times when I became very curious in my walk with God — times when I wanted to know more about having a relationship with the Lord Jesus Christ and how to make it a reality in my life. I wanted a relationship that went far beyond the initial moment of salvation, one that would create in me a desire to know the Bible — and not just intellectually. I also wanted to know the Bible experientially by applying it to my life. I wanted to be able to live the Bible and see its teachings work in my life.

Consumed

After two years on the path of confusion and curiosity in my Christian life, I finally arrived at the leg of my spiritual journey I call the "consuming heart." It is here that you finally get off dead center and turn the corner with Christianity. It is here, when reality sets in, that you understand that Christianity *does* work! It is here, when your heart is consumed with God, that you realize the head-to-head communication style in your relationships isn't going to work. You realize this style will soon fail and produce only a miserable life filled with conflict, pain, resentment, and quite probably broken relationships.

On the positive side, it is at this point that you begin to believe Christianity really does work, and you begin to communicate in a heart-to-heart manner. You become consumed with seeing where Christianity will take you on your journey, and you finally experience authentic Christianity in your relationships. When you are consumed with the Bible, God, Jesus Christ, and the Holy Spirit, you begin to realize life isn't about you and your ego. Instead, it's about God.

Consumed Defined

The word *consumed* has many different definitions. I want to make it clear that when I use the word *consumed*, I'm using the definition that means "to fill one's mind and heart fully with the things of God." It means to be engrossed completely and absorbed fully with your spiritual relationship with God. It means to have your mind and heart completely occupied with God. The two men on the road to Emmaus were consumed with Jesus when their eyes were opened, and they said, "Did not our heart burn within us?" The Greek word for *burn* is *kaio*, which means "to ignite" or "set on fire."[9]

When I was experiencing a corrupt and confused heart, my mind wasn't on the things of God; it was selfishly only on myself. As a matter of fact, when I was in a state of confusion, I didn't want to read the Bible, and I didn't want to pray, and if I hadn't been the pastor, I probably wouldn't have attended church services. "Why?" you may ask. The reason I was so negative about the things of God was simply that I was consumed with only myself and what I was experiencing.

Consumed Illustrated

Let me share a story with you found in Luke 24. It's about two men who took a journey, much like we might take. They were walking on the road to Emmaus following the events of the death, burial, and resurrection of Jesus Christ. The two individuals in this story experienced the three different emotions I've discussed in this chapter. As they were walking down the road, they were headed away from all the activity that had taken place. They were going toward the city of Emmaus and no doubt were sad and had

---

[9] *Strong's Concordance,* http://biblehub.com/greek/2545.htm

confused hearts. They were talking about all the events that had recently happened to Jesus, who incidentally was the one they had believed would be the redeemer of Israel.

As they were walking and talking, Jesus came alongside them and asked what they were talking about and why they were so sad. They said to Him, "Are you the only stranger in Jerusalem, and have you not known the things which happened there in these days?" (Luke 24:18 NKJV) They didn't even recognize Jesus as He walked beside them. You see, their dreams had been crushed, and their hopes had been dashed. Because of this disappointment, they were confused and couldn't even recognize Jesus.

This situation is very similar to times when our dreams are crushed and our hopes are dashed; we become so confused that we can't see Jesus clearly. Because of our confusion, we wander around and have no sense of direction on our journey. All we can do is simply wonder what in the world is going on in our lives.

The farther those two men traveled with Jesus, the more their journey changed to something much better. Instead of sad hearts, they now experienced slow and curious hearts. Their curiosity suddenly was aroused.

The same change of heart can happen to us; yes, we may be confused about what is happening, but there's also something intriguing happening in our lives, and we're curious. We want to find out what it is that's so intriguing.

The story in Luke continues with the two men recounting the recent events in Jerusalem. They said that some of the women from their group had gone to the tomb early in the morning and returned with an amazing report. The women said Jesus's body was missing, and they'd seen angels who had told them Jesus was alive! Some of their men ran out to see, and sure enough, Jesus's body was gone.

Their curiosity was about to open up a whole new segment on their journey. Even though they still didn't clearly see that Jesus was walking alongside them, they were about to see Him as they had never seen Him before — and they were about to burn inside with consuming hearts. They begged Jesus to stay the night with them since it was late, so He went home with them. As they sat down to eat, Jesus took a small loaf of bread, asked God's blessing on it, broke it, and gave it to them. At that moment their eyes were suddenly opened, and they recognized Him. They said to each other, "Did not our hearts burn within us as he talked to us and explained the Scripture?"

Notice the beauty of how God works in the journey of our lives. During their travel on the road to Emmaus, the men first had sad or confused hearts. Next they had slow or curious hearts; and finally, when they saw Jesus, they had burning or consuming hearts. Their hearts went from confused to curious to consuming.

Consumed Experienced

The same sequence of emotions often takes place in our spiritual life journey and in our relationship with Christ. Because we have what I call "junk" in our lives, we cannot see Jesus clearly. In turn, this produces disappointment, hurt, pain, and failure, so we become confused. In the midst of this confusion, an event will suddenly take place in our lives. This event usually grabs our attention, and we become curious as to what is going on around us, even though we may not completely understand what's happening.

If we continue on our journey of curiosity and refuse to give up, eventually we'll reach the point where our spiritual eyes are opened to the purpose behind the circumstances in our lives. Our spiritual eyes begin to focus on reality, and suddenly we see Jesus more clearly. We see Him as we've never seen Him before. It isn't a matter of knowing more facts about Him but coming to the place where we truly *know* Him in a real and authentic way.

It is at this consuming juncture of our spiritual journey that a change begins to take place. At this point the journey begins to change from the "head" to the "heart" way of life. The journey inches its way forward, leading us to experience a more pleasant, pleasing, productive Christian life by creating within us a changing heart.

Remember, the most difficult spiritual journey we will ever take is the eighteen inches from the head to the heart. That eighteen-inch journey meanders its way through the hills, valleys, curves, and potholes of a confused, curious, consuming heart until we reach the destination of a changed and clean heart.

***Consumed* Transforms**

Possibly for the first time in our lives, we can be real and authentic with our Christianity. We no longer have to wear a mask, pretending we have it all together. We no longer have to try to make people think everything is just fine with our lives. We finally reach the point Jesus talks about so often in the Bible, where we can live in joy, peace, and tranquility — and truly experience the abundant life. When we're consumed with God and reach this point, we can let loose of ourselves; we no longer have to feed our egos; and we no longer have to play games. We can also begin to eliminate most of the fighting, fussing, and feuding in our relationships.

This will be the point in your Christian life when you have an encounter with God that finds you wrestling with Him and not willing to let go until He blesses you very much, like the encounter Jacob had at Peniel when he wrestled with God. Jacob was consumed with God so much that he was willing to leave Peniel only after God had blessed him; he was willing to leave injured and spend the rest of his life limping. After this encounter Jacob made it very clear that he was consumed with God when he said, "For I have seen God face to face, and my life is preserved" (Gen. 32:30b). I believe this is the journey most Christians want to take in their lives. Have you ever come to the place where you were willing to wrestle with God no matter what the outcome might be?

In our Christian journey, I see similarities to the experiences the apostle Paul expressed; I discussed these earlier in this book. He was confused in one sense, because of the sinful things he didn't want to do as a Christian; nevertheless he found himself doing them. On the other side of the coin, the good things he wanted to do as a Christian he couldn't make himself do. He was stymied in his spiritual life and couldn't move forward until something drastic happened.

Even though Paul was confused, he apparently became curious about his spiritual life, because he spoke about being delighted in the transformation that was taking place inside him. Notice the statement he made concerning his curiosity: "For I delight in the law of God after the inward man" (Rom. 7:22). Paul knew there was something more, something greater for him than just the physical part of his life. In much of the Book of Romans, he shared with us about this curiosity that stimulated his inner life and advanced his spiritual life.

In Romans Paul shared his findings with us; he became consumed with the Lord Jesus Christ. He said, "For the law of the Spirit of life in Christ Jesus hath made me free from the law of sin and death" (Rom. 8:2). He experienced that spiritual principle of one law overriding another law — in other words one principle overriding another principle, such as the law of aerodynamics overriding the law of gravity. I believe Paul was consumed with analyzing how the law of the Spirit of life in Christ transformed and changed his heart and ultimately his behavior.

Paul was so consumed with Christ that he made the following statement: "No, dear brothers and sisters, I have not achieved it, but I focus on this one thing: Forgetting the past and looking forward to what lies ahead, I press on to reach the end of the race and receive the heavenly prize for which God, through Christ Jesus, is calling us" (Phil. 3:13–14 NLT).

Paul stated that he continued to be curious because he wasn't yet where he should have been spiritually. However, he wasn't willing to remain on that leg of his journey, because he was now consumed with and focused on one thing. That one thing was having his energies be fully occupied with — and his inner man looking at — what lay ahead for him; he strained toward the end of the race to receive the prize.

No matter who we are or how spiritual we may think we are, we all desperately need change in our spiritual lives and in our relationship with Christ. Change, of course, isn't an easy thing to accept. The reason is that it takes the process discussed in this chapter to make it happen. We don't want our hearts to travel down the road of confusion, curiosity, or consumption, because change takes time and usually involves dealing with our inner person or, more specifically, our egos.

This is one leg of your journey you can leave with a real sense of accomplishment and be pleased with the outcome of your journey thus far. At this point you can sit back and be in awe at what you've seen, much like when I was in awe seeing Niagara Falls, the Grand Canyon, and Old Faithful.

You have finally come to the point where you've wrestled with God and now can see Jesus clearly and stand in awe of Him. You can now say, as the two men on the road to Emmaus did, "Didn't our hearts burn within us?" This is the experience of this chapter that will take us to the next leg of our journey, which is the changed heart.

Don't get discouraged if you haven't arrived at this point yet. As the apostle Paul reminded us, just keep pressing toward the mark.

Part 3
Live the Victory

Defying the Potholes

It's very possible that as we've experienced the potholes of Christianity, we've been so beaten down that we don't think we have the right to live a life of victory. The potholes will always be in existence. They will never be eliminated or deleted from Christianity. They will never go away. They are a reality.

The last three chapters of this book speak of victory. A changing heart, a clean heart, and a contrite heart are the means to defying the potholes of Christianity. The arena of life is where you win the battle and become the victor. You stand eyeball to eyeball with the potholes and are able to defy them in the name of Jesus Christ, who has changed your heart to one that is clean and contrite.

Enjoy these chapters, and accept and receive the victory God has given you. No matter the failures you've experienced in the potholes of Christianity, God's grace will lift you out of them and is sufficient to enable you to walk in victory for the rest of your life.

Chapter 9
A Changed Heart

Therefore also now, sayeth the Lord, turn ye even to me with all your heart, and with fasting, and with weeping, and with mourning: and rend your hearts, and not your garments, and turn unto the Lord your God: for he is gracious and merciful, slow to anger, and of great kindness, and repenteth him of the evil.
—*Joel 2:12–13*

Create in me a clean heart, O God; and renew a right spirit within me.
—*Ps. 51:10*

And the Lord said, Simon, Simon, behold, Satan hath desired to have you, that he may sift you as wheat: But I have prayed for thee, that thy faith fail not: and when thou art converted, strengthen thy brethren.
—*Luke 22:31–32*

This segment of our spiritual journey is, no doubt, the most difficult segment we will face as we grow in the grace and knowledge of our Lord Jesus Christ. If we ever decided we were through with Christianity and wanted to end our journey with God, it would be at this point that change would need to take place in our lives. Change isn't something we're comfortable with. We don't like to talk about change; in fact we want nothing to do with change because it takes us out of our comfort zones and can be very painful. Change demands that we replace the love of ourselves with the love of God. Change, as I've mentioned before, is a shocking blow to our egos.

However, it is at this juncture of our journey that we finally find the answer to the question we asked in chapter one. Does Christianity work? When you reach this point and are willing to travel through this "changed-heart" community, you will experience the ultimate fact that Christianity *does* work. Not only does it work, but it can also fulfill its many promises stated in the word of God.

Here at the "changed-heart" community, you will find a sense of peace for your life. You will no longer have to live with head-to-head, confrontational battles in all your relationships. For the very first time in your life, you will be able to experience and deal with your relationships on a heart-to-heart basis. It is here that you will truly understand what the Bible means when it says, "For out of it are the issues of life" (Prov. 4:23b). This is where the eighteen-inch journey from the head to the heart comes to an end and is completed. The wondrous knowledge of the word of God, which you possess in your mind, will now be transformed, transferred, and assimilated into your heart. It will then be dispersed outwardly in your various relationships in a kind, loving way. Everyone you are associated with will be able to see this change in your life.

This is the very reason I had to include chapter two of this book. While writing that chapter, it seemed like a very negative way to begin a book. If you recall, chapter two is subtitled "Why Is There Strife in Our Lives?" Now we can see that the reason for the strife is that we have the tendency to live from the head rather than from the heart. To eliminate this strife from our lives, change is required, and that change requires that we begin to live from the heart.

In Psalm 51:10, David, a man after God's own heart, said, "Create in me a clean heart, O God; and renew a right spirit within me." And in verse 12, he said, "Restore unto me the joy of thy salvation; and uphold me with thy free spirit." To sum it up, David told God he was tired of living a life filled with conflict and wanted to change. Many Christians today are tired, worn out, ready to give up, and are experiencing this very same kind of conflict. They are tired of conflict, legalism, hypocrisy, judgmental people, meanspirited attitudes, and downright angry people who consider themselves to be brothers and sisters in the Lord.

Our churches in America, and even those around the world, are in desperate need of change in the lives of God's people who attend these churches. God means for our attitudes and the way we live to be like a magnet, pulling people into a relationship with Christ and with their church, but instead we're pushing the lost even farther away with our negative lives.

Let's look closely at what this change might consist of and what is actually required for change to take place in our lives. I believe we can picture this change in our lives with the following descriptions. Never underestimate what God is able to do when He works in our lives. His desire, goal, and work are for us to experience a change in our spiritual lives.

A Rended Heart

And rend your heart, and not your garments.
—Joel 2:13

The Hebrew culture has always included the rending of garments to show repentance, regret, grief, and sorrow. Jewish people often tore their garments and girded themselves with sackcloth. In the Scripture above, God was telling them he'd had enough of their outward expression. He wanted them to rend their hearts, which is an inward experience. I guarantee you that it would have been easier for them to rend their garments than their hearts.

David defined the rending of the heart after asking God to forgive him for his sin, which reminds us that a true rending of the heart is as stated: "The sacrifices of God are a broken spirit: a broken and contrite heart, O God, thou wilt not despise" (Ps. 51:17).

Since sin has so hardened our hearts, it's easy to see why it's so difficult for our hearts to be torn and changed. This is why the entire process seems so painful. You see, the Holy Spirit works and tugs at our hardened hearts. This rending takes place deep in our souls and is a heartfelt and extremely humiliating experience. This rending brings forth a cleansing deep in our souls and prepares us to have the fruit of the Spirit released from our lives in the future. When you experience the brokenness of your heart through the work of the Holy Spirit, your mind and heart begin to open up to the things of God. That brings us to the next point, a converted heart, which I believe many born-again Christians have never truly experienced.

A Converted Heart

But I have prayed for thee, that thy faith fail not: and when thou art converted, strengthen thy brethren.
—*Luke 22:32*

Before Peter became a follower of Christ, he lived in a state of great earthly satisfaction, and I'm sure he enjoyed being a fisherman. Once he found Christ and was regenerated, however, he turned from his carnal and secular ways, became a fisher of men, and grew in his spiritual faith. As we read his story in the Bible, we find him in a position where he allowed his ego and heart to take control of his life.

We often find ourselves in this same position; when this happens, we're doomed for failure in our spiritual lives. Peter was going to do some things that, from a biblical point of view, made it look as if he weren't a Christian at all. When the multitudes confronted Jesus in the garden, Peter took a sword and cut off the ear of one of the high priest's servants. Later Peter followed the Lord from afar and sat among the Lord's enemies. Finally, his action of denying the Lord was as diabolical as he could get.

Jesus warned Peter that he would have a conflict with Satan in the future, that his faith would be tested, and that he would fail for a period of time. Jesus explained that when that testing happened, and when Peter would travel through that painful time in his life, Jesus would be with him. But Peter would have to experience a change in his heart and life.

Think back for a moment to when we began our journey in the initial pages of this book. Though our sins may be different from Peter's, we certainly can relate to the fact that we need to change from our head-to-head confrontations. We must stop our fighting and fussing, put away our meanspirited actions toward other Christians, and eliminate our negative way of life. These sins cause us to carry into the church a church-dividing attitude that makes us think we're entitled to something special from the church. You see, there are times when we can cut off an ear with a sharp tongue, using sharp words, or we can keep our distance far from Jesus so we can be identified with him slightly but certainly not too noticeably as a Christian. In a subtle way with our unchristian behavior, we're denying our Lord as Peter did during his painful experience.

There comes a time in our lives when we must turn away from our past, run to God, and grow in Him once again. That growth comes from the rending and brokenness of our hearts. This point is known as conversion, a turning or returning to the almighty Lord.

Notice how this very thing was brought about in Peter's life. Satan was allowed to sift Peter like wheat. The Lord didn't tell Peter that He would rescue him and get him out of the situation; rather He simply said He would pray for Peter. Peter had to go through the painful process and experience the rending and brokenness of his heart before he could become what God wanted him to be.

In Luke 22:32, Jesus said, "But I have prayed for thee, that thy faith fail not." The word *fail* comes from the Greek word *ecleipo*, from which we get our English word *eclipse*. Peter's faith was like an eclipse of the moon, when it is dark for a time but eventually illuminated once again. What Peter was about to do in his denial meant that his faith would be darkened for a season, and those around him wouldn't see his faith or its influence. However, when his heart was changed, his faith would be illuminated again, because he would be converted or, in other words, changed. The word *converted* simply means "turned," "changed," or "recovered."

There are many painful situations or siftings we experience in our lives that can become a true source of spiritual growth in the long run. If you look at those situations as an opportunity for God to work in your life and bring change in your life, you will see them in a more positive way and will probably have a more positive outcome. Make no mistake about it — times can be hard, and it can be difficult to look at certain situations in that light. But I'm telling you that through the rending and sifting of our lives, God is able to convert, bring change, and transform our hearts from corrupt hearts to clean hearts. This should be the desire of every Christian on the face of the earth.

At this point Christianity becomes real. It becomes real because your spiritual eyes have been opened to the fact that you can truly practice the word of God in your daily life. Your relationships will flourish and will be unlike any you've experienced before, because you will be able to communicate on a heart-to-heart basis rather than on a head-to-head basis. You may wonder why it's only now that you can understand and practice Christianity. The answer to that question is that the eyes of your understanding have been opened.

When the apostle Paul wrote to the Christians at Ephesus, he stated in his letter:

> That the God of our Lord Jesus Christ, the Father of glory, may give you the Spirit of wisdom and of revelation in the knowledge of Him, having the eyes of your hearts enlightened, that you may know what is the hope to which He has called you, what are the riches of His glorious inheritance in the saints, and what is the immeasurable greatness of His power toward us who believe, according to the working of his great might. (Eph. 1:17–19 ESV)

The Holy Spirit of God illuminates our minds so that we may understand biblical principles and apply them to our lives.

We now have reached the point in our journey where we can begin to see how Christianity truly works. We've seen the transformation of moving from a corrupt and confused heart to one that is being cleansed through fire. With this the issues of life that proceed out of our hearts will now be pure and clean. There is a feeling of finally being released from the bondage of the past. It's a 360-degree turn in our Christian lives. Now, instead of all the rubbish that has been pouring out of our lives, we will begin to see the fruit of the Spirit flowing in a natural way, without our efforts, from our hearts, and bearing the fruits of peace, joy, love, and tranquility. Having traveled this long, painful journey, we have officially come to the place where God has intended us to arrive: living with a clean and pure heart for Him and those we relate to.

A Changed Heart

But we all, with open face beholding as in a glass the glory of the Lord, are changed into the same image from glory to glory, even as by the Sprit of the Lord.
—*2 Cor. 3:18*

When we reach the point where we've been changed into His image, and His life flows through us by the power and influence of the Spirit of God, then we can be witnesses to strengthen our brothers and sisters in Christ.

Can you imagine how much different life would be and the freedom we would experience if our hearts were changed and transformed, as described in the Book of Galatians?

> When you follow the desires of your sinful nature, the results are very clear: sexual immorality, impurity, lustful pleasures, idolatry, sorcery, hostility, quarreling, jealousy, outbursts of anger, selfish ambition, dissension, division,

envy, drunkenness, wild parties, and other sins like these. Let me tell you again, as I have before, that anyone living that sort of life will not inherit the Kingdom of God. But the Holy Spirit produces this kind of fruit in our lives: love, joy, peace, patience, kindness, goodness, faithfulness, gentleness, and self-control. There is no law against these things! (Gal. 5:19-23 NLT)

How much more at peace we would be if we were converted and changed from living life in the flesh to living life in the Spirit? Can you imagine how much different our marriages, families, and churches would be if our hearts were changed? Remember, from out of the heart are the issues of life. Notice in these verses that two different ways of life and two different patterns are portrayed. Take a close look and determine which way of life you would like to live and experience in the future.

God makes it very clear with His wording that if we choose to live according to the flesh, it will produce sin in our lives. Sin will produce sinful attitudes and sinful behavior. Let me mention a few words in this list: *quarreling, jealousy, outburst of anger, selfishness,* and *divisions.* They define the baggage we bring into our marriages, families, and churches. When we choose to live in the Spirit, however, the picture changes and is refreshingly different; the wording is pleasant and peaceful. A changed heart brings a heart-to-heart attitude into our various relationships.

The image referred to above in 2 Corinthians 3:18 is one in which we're changed into the likeness of Christ; we will live in the midst of the fruit of the Spirit. Consequently, as He produces this fruit in us, instead of bringing baggage into our relationships, we will in a natural way bring spiritual fruit into each relationship.

You see, Christians' lives never plateau, for we're moving either forward or backward. Because God will never allow us to remain on a plateau, He will work in our lives to bring change to our hearts and draw us closer and closer to Him. A changed heart, then, is the avenue to the next leg of our journey: a clean heart. This is God's destination for each and every one of us who has become a Christian. His desire is for us to experience the peace and joy of living with a clean heart.

Chapter 10
A Clean Heart

Create in me a clean heart, O God; and renew a right spirit within me.
—Ps. 51:10

    While traveling you will find that your journey will take you from city to city, and you will see that the overall condition of each city will vary considerably. I recall a city in Europe I visited for ten days; it was extremely dirty, dark, and drab. The electricity was limited to the extent that only occasionally would I see a streetlight or porch light on at night. The main buildings in the city, if painted at all, had been painted with dark, dull colors. While driving our car, we had to dodge deep, wide potholes in the middle of the streets. It was so depressing that I couldn't wait until I was able to leave that city and experience a change of scenery.

    On the other hand, in my travels I have driven into many cities — some small and some large — that were very colorful, dressed up with paint, and adorned with hanging plants and flowers. The streets were clean and attractive and as smooth as glass. I enjoyed them so much that I wanted to stay and visit for a while just to enjoy the setting.

    I just described geographical journeys I took that are similar to the spiritual journey I've taken. You can probably relate to such a journey; if not, I'm sure you will have such a journey sometime in the future. The differences between the images of the two cities represent the images of the journey you will take from a corrupt heart to a clean one. Once your journey takes you to a clean, spiritual heart, I guarantee you will want to stay and visit there just to enjoy the setting and the surroundings of a clean heart.

As we've been traveling on our spiritual life journey, which started in chapter one, you can see the ultimate goal for us is to end that journey with a clean heart. We want a heart that is absent of dirty, dark, drab, sinful surroundings; we want it changed to a heart that is attractive, clean, colorful, appealing, and pleasant to be around and reside in.

David found himself on a spiritual journey in which his heart had become dirty and dark because of the sin he had committed; at the time he'd ignored that sin and was living life as though nothing had happened. Well, in reality it did happen, and his heart was dirty because of the sin he'd committed against God when he had an affair with Bathsheba. Consequently that affair caused pain, hurt, and heartache for many people with whom he had relationships.

David's heart wasn't clean at that moment, and though he tried to ignore the sin, it was ever present and polluted his heart. It wasn't until Nathan exposed David's sin that David finally acknowledged how dirty his heart really was. Even though he was a man after God's own heart, he was also a human being capable of this sin, and he'd gone astray. The entirety of Psalm 51 records David's prayer of repentance, in which he asked God to create in him a clean heart.

David's sin started out in his heart, and his heart ruled over his mind. Then his will was set into motion by his making the wrong decision. Because of that decision, he committed adultery, which led to other sins, as he tried to hide and cover up his original sin. *From out of the heart are the issues of life.* Everything issues forth from the heart; because of this fact, we must take the journey to have a clean heart.

We may think we could never commit adultery, as David did with Bathsheba. I would say, lest we become overconfident in our abilities not to sin, we should take a moment and consider where our hearts are at the present time with God. We must consider what's going round and round in our minds that could very well be a time bomb ready to go off, causing us to make that decision to sin against God.

You see, sin sours and contaminates our hearts. When we're backslidden, as David was, we become irritable, testy, grumpy, disagreeable, critical, and judgmental. And we're quick to attack other people. We feel extremely dirty in the heart and become so miserable that we try to take the pain we're experiencing and transfer it to other people — usually to the people we love the most. While living this life with unclean hearts, we do everything possible to deny our heart's condition. This is why we aren't willing to be transformed in our lives or to be transparent in our relationships. This is the reason we would rather use a head-to-head style of communication in our relationships than in a heart-to-heart style.

David knew that through his own efforts his heart could never be clean. He realized that only through the power of the Holy Spirit of God could he ever experience a clean heart. It is absolutely necessary for us to know that we cannot cleanse our own hearts. Our cleansing will come only through the mighty act of God working in our lives. Take a moment to read Psalm 51 and see David crying out to God to create in him a clean heart and to renew a right spirit within him.

We often think that if we can change our way of life by changing our thinking patterns and behavior, everything will be OK. At this point we read the Bible more frequently, get up earlier in the morning to pray longer, attend church more frequently, and believe everything will automatically change. Though these are natural, scriptural, and good things to do after searching our souls, we must be reminded as David was and come to the conclusion that God and God alone can cleanse our hearts.

David's prayer was simply for God to create in him a clean heart. When we think of the word *create*, we often think of God forming something out of nothing. The Hebrew word for *create* is sometimes defined as "making something out of nothing." However, there are times when *create* simply means "to shape, fashion, or reform something or someone."[10] I believe this is its meaning in regard to God's dealing with David's heart. David was asking God to reform, shape, and fashion his heart into a clean, transformed heart.

David wasn't talking about some momentary operation taking place in his life, like when he came to know God, but rather a work that was continually taking place in his daily life. We might think of "work" in terms of not only that moment in which we were saved but also a work that constantly takes place in our daily lives. The cleansing work of God is a day-by-day work He began in our lives the moment we received Him as our Savior.

We can see this same daily cleansing pattern portrayed in the New Testament when the apostle Paul, writing to the church at Philippi, spoke of the confidence he had in God's daily work in his life. Notice what Paul said: "Being confident of this very thing, that He which hath begun a good work in you will perform it until the day of Jesus Christ" (Phil. 1:6). He said that God began a good work, or a cleansing work, in him when he came to know Christ personally and that God would perform that work in him until Jesus came again. In Philippians 2:13 (ESV) Paul went on

---

10 *Brown-Driver-Briggs Hebrew and English Lexicon;* Francis Brown, Samuel Rolles Driver, Charles A. Briggs; Snowball Publishing; 2010

to say, "For God is working in you, giving you the desire and the power to do what pleases him." He spoke of that continual, daily, progressive work of sanctification that takes place in our lives and cleanses us as only the Holy Spirit of God can. Paul made it clear that it is God who works in you to give you that desire to do His will and enables or empowers you to work for His good pleasure or His will.

Again David knew he couldn't be cleansed without the mighty works of God in his heart. It is of utmost importance that we quickly reach the same understanding David did — that at this point God is able to cleanse our hearts once we get out of His way and allow Him to do His work in us. Incidentally it is the pain of this journey that brings us to this understanding.

The one thing David desired the most, while confessing his sin to God and acknowledging the sin he'd committed against God, was for his heart to be clean.

The word *clean* means "purified" or "to become pure," which is the opposite of a dirty or contaminated heart. It doesn't mean sinless perfection or imply that we will never sin again, but it does mean that one's life is changing and being transformed from a corrupt heart to a clean and pure heart. *Clean* speaks of a transformed heart, in which the fruit of the Spirit overcomes and overshadows the works of the flesh. To measure the progress in our spiritual journey, we can take the works of the flesh and the fruit of the Spirit, as listed in Galatians 5:19–23, and put them on God's balancing scales. This will show us whether we're progressing in our spiritual lives. In other words does the fruit of the Spirit outweigh the works of the flesh in our lives?

David asked for a clean, pure heart, which would be pleasing to God and very beneficial to David himself. Think of the blessings he would experience once God cleansed his heart. Think of the burden released and the lifting of the weight from his soul he must have experienced after he opened his heart to God and confessed his sin. I believe David made this request to God with a broken and contrite heart. Allowing God to cleanse our hearts brings some very real benefits to our lives.

In the Sermon on the Mount, Jesus spoke of the blessings of a clean heart in the section known as the Beatitudes. Jesus said, "Blessed are the pure in heart: for they shall see God" (Matt. 5:8). The phrase "in heart" speaks of an inward purity that will open our inward eyes so that we may be able to see God more clearly. A pure heart isn't a heart that is dark, scummy, or clouded over with anger, jealousy, envy, bitterness, unforgiveness, arrogance, or a multitude of other sinful attitudes and behaviors. With such attitudes and behaviors, we cannot see God clearly. A pure heart is filled with love, joy, peace, long-suffering, gentleness, goodness, faith, meekness, and temperance. It is one that allows us to see God very clearly.

At this final leg of the journey, you will be able to settle down and see God more clearly. Here you will find the rest, peace, joy, and satisfaction you've been looking for, maybe for years. At this stage you will experience the exchanged life: His life for yours. Here you will experience not only life but also the abundant life Jesus promises to the believer.

In the following verses, the apostles Paul and Peter spoke of the rewards and blessings of a pure and clean heart in all your relationships.

A Clear Conscience

Don't let them waste their time in endless discussion of myths and spiritual pedigrees. These things only lead to meaningless speculations, which don't help people live a life of faith in

God. The purpose of my instruction is that all believers would be filled with love that comes from a pure heart, a clear conscience, and genuine faith.
—1Tim. 1:4–5 NLT

A Calling on the Lord

Run from anything that stimulates youthful lust. Instead, pursue righteous living, faithfulness, love, and peace. Enjoy the companionship of those who call on the Lord with pure hearts.
—2 Tim. 2:22 NLT

A Genuine Love

Now that you have purified yourselves by obeying the truth so that you have sincere love for each other, love one another deeply, from the heart.
—1 Pet. 1:22 NIV

In the verses above, we find that pure hearts will stimulate love and clear our consciences of evildoings. A pure heart will make us want to do what's right vertically in our relationships with God and horizontally with other people. It will provide peace so we can enjoy fellowship not only with God but also with our spouses, families, church members, and coworkers.

When you compare a clean heart with a corrupt heart, which I described in a previous chapter, you can see there is a huge gap between the two.

It's a gap between a flintlike, hardened heart and a very soft heart; a gap between an extremely wicked heart and a decent heart; a gap between a deceitful heart and an honest heart with a clear conscience. The difference between the two hearts represents a transformation that takes place in our hearts only by the grace and power of God.

At the very center of Christianity is the cross of the Lord Jesus Christ. The cross is what stands between the heavens and the earth, bringing the two together in harmony. Keep in mind how the vertical and horizontal bars come together to form the cross. That cross requires love and attention toward God and our relationship with Him, as well as love and attention toward other people and our relationships with them.

At this juncture everything comes together in your Christian life and in the realm of your relationships. At this juncture the vertical and horizontal meet. It is much like when we look at where the vertical and horizontal bars meet on the cross. This is important because where these two bars meet, we have the whole, and we have harmony. We must keep these two things — the vertical and horizontal relationships — in harmony with each other.

When our vertical relationship with God isn't clean and pure, our horizontal relationships with each other won't be clean and pure. If our relationships with each other aren't pure, our relationship with God won't be clean and pure. There are times when we're truly and strictly focused on our vertical relationship with God. These times are vital to the overall growth of our spiritual lives.

Then there are times when we're more focused on our horizontal relationships. These times provide growth in our personal relationships. However, there comes a time when the vertical and the horizontal relationships meet, and it is here where we find, through clean hearts, the peace and tranquility we all desire for our lives so much.

A Clean Heart

In the advertising world, we hear phrases tossed around in an attempt to sell a product, such as "pure sugar," "pure silver," "pure gold," "pure water," or "purebred." *Pure* actually means something meets a standard of quality and isn't contaminated or mixed with any other substance. I can't think of a greater advertisement for Christianity than for God's people to possess clean and pure hearts. We can be God's advertising agents, telling the world that God's people can get along in their families, in their nation, and in their churches.

We should be the ones advertising that Christianity does work. I believe the greatest selling point for Christianity is for the world to see that we've traveled on our journey from a corrupt heart to a clean and pure heart. Remember, from out of the heart come the issues of life. When those in the world see such a life, deep down they really want what we have in Christ Jesus. They have no tolerance for the fighting, fussing, and carrying-on they so often see Christians producing; rather they are drawn to people who extend grace to them through the peace, joy, and tranquility of their clean hearts.

The journey we've spoken of in this book is an eighteen-inch journey of becoming what God wants us to be. You see, God is more concerned about our "becoming" than our "doing." God never intended us to remain paralyzed with corrupt hearts. He intends for us to change and become clean vessels for His use through our clean hearts. This is when Christianity becomes enjoyable and satisfying to us. Now we'll be able to serve Him because we've first become what God wants us to be. You can serve and never "become," which will lead to burnout in your ministry and sometimes a complete meltdown in Christianity itself. On the other hand, if you first "become," then you will automatically do, and you will serve with gladness, never thinking of burning out in ministry.

This is a great place to end the journey. When you make the journey from the head to the heart, it will take you from a corrupt heart to a clean heart. When you finally reach the destination of a clean heart, your experience will be much like returning home after traveling throughout the United States. You will have peace and contentment regarding your trip. It will be like unpacking your suitcases, going through a couple of weeks of mail, listening to the messages on your voice mail, flipping through the brochures and magazines, sitting back in your favorite recliner in a state of peace and contentment, and reflecting on the success of your journey. Most important, you will be able to sleep in the comfort of your own bed.

Every journey you make has a starting point and ultimately an ending point. When you begin a trip, you hope and desire that when you come to the end of that trip, you will have enjoyed it tremendously. You hope the information, beauty, and experience of that trip will have changed your life. While traveling you may have experienced times when you were tired or lost, had to ask for directions, or had car problems after hitting one of the potholes on the highway. Or you may have gotten upset with the children in the backseat or had not been able to find a motel room to stay in on short notice. Despite all the frustrations of the trip, you're sitting in your easy chair, saying, "It was well worth the trip."

I've heard the questions many times: "How do I apply the word of God to my life?" "Why doesn't the Christian life work for me?" "Why are my relationships always filled with drama and conflicts?" "Does Christianity really work in our lives?" "Why am I so confused about Christianity?" "Why doesn't my life line up with the word of God?"

In the final chapter of this book, I would like to address what I believe is the key to making the successful journey from the head to the heart — or, to say it another way, the journey from a corrupt heart to a clean heart.

The key is a broken and contrite heart. Oh, yes, it's the key. You need the key to start the journey. Put the key in the ignition switch of your spiritual journey, and let's get started on the eighteen-inch journey of your spiritual life.

Chapter 11

A Contrite Heart

For thou desirest not sacrifice; else would I give it; thou delightest not in burnt offering. The sacrifices of God are a broken spirit: a broken and a contrite heart, O God, thou wilt not despise.
—Ps. 51:16–17 (emphasis added)

When we reach the point of having a clean heart, the greatest question we must have answered is "How did we get here after meandering our way through each leg of our spiritual journey?" Each segment seems to have given us a few answers to the questions we may have about our journey. Eventually we arrive at the point or destination where God wanted us all along, which is to live with a clean heart. However, once we've arrived at our destination with a clean heart, we still have that gnawing question that keeps dogging us: "Now I have a sense of peace, joy, purpose, and direction in my life that I've never had before. But how did I get to this place where Christianity does work in my life?"

This last chapter will answer the following questions for you: "Does Christianity work?" and "How did I get from a corrupt heart to the destination of a clean heart?" Our Scripture makes it very clear that God doesn't desire any sacrifice from us or delight in any burned offerings we might present to Him to appease Him. What He *does* delight in is when He is able to approve, think highly of, and value our contrite hearts or what we may call our broken hearts.

You see, God places great value on a contrite heart. It is the broken and contrite heart that answers these questions for each and every one of us. A contrite heart produces humility in our lives, which deals a tremendous blow to our egos. Keep in mind that, from the very beginning, the Bible teaches, "From out of the heart are the issues of life." God looks not on the outer person but on the heart.

You see, salvation isn't a process but an instantaneous once-and-for-all occasion. Your spiritual life journey may have been a process of learning intellectually about salvation up to the point when you were saved, but salvation itself isn't a process. You are saved or become a follower of Christ the minute you receive Him into your life and the Holy Spirit comes to dwell within you.

However, after you become a follower of Christ, your Christian life journey then becomes a process. Your salvation progresses forward, and you should grow in your Christian life until the day you die. It is this spiritual growth, which is often in conflict with our flesh, that creates the greatest obstacles in our lives. It is in the growth stage and process that we find the most confusion, frustration, and often the most pain. As new followers of Christ, we believe naïvely — or spiritual leaders have taught us to believe — that immediately after we become Christians, our lives will be without problems, issues, or painful events. In other words we're taught that life will be lived in a utopia, an ideal and perfect place. Really, do you think that's true?

Sometimes our egos take over, and we believe we're now extremely spiritual beings, and nothing can touch us. We go around with a facade on our faces, making everyone think we have no negative or sinful issues in life — when in fact we do have issues, and sometimes they create dysfunctional lives.

This final chapter focuses on our understanding three principles of spiritual-life growth and how our hearts journey to the place where we do experience victory and abundance in our everyday Christian lives. And yes, I'm finding peace and joy in my daily journey. And yes, Christianity is working in my life.

Not only do we want this victory in our lives, but because of our understanding of the process, we will also have patience with other people to help them as they continue to make their journey from chapter to chapter. I'm going to emphasize the following three principles God teaches. We need to know, understand, and remember them during our journey if we're to experience victory, peace, and joy in our spiritual growth and really understand how we got to the place of a clean heart in our Christian lives.

The first principle we'll look at deals with the process. This is a relatively easy principle to understand and practice when we break it down into two segments.

The Process of Our Growth

It is imperative that you study, memorize, know, and understand the word of God. Without information from the word of God, you will never find the map God has laid out for your spiritual journey, and you will never find the direction in which He is leading you on this journey. I'm convinced about the two words I'm going to talk about at this point, and my humble understanding of these two words made a great impact on my life by bringing about a great change in my heart. I wish I'd had this knowledge earlier in my life, for it would have saved me from many painful experiences. It wasn't until I was in my midforties, however, that these two words came across the path of my journey. From that point until this very day, I've had the joy of growing in the Lord.

Appropriation

Just because you see words on the pages of the Bible as you read doesn't mean they have any effect on your spiritual life. You may not be *appropriating* the word of God to your life; you may be only *reading* the word of God. *Appropriation* means that you claim by faith every word and every promise from the Bible for your life and make that word and promise your own. These words become yours when you allow them to activate your faith.

For years my thinking was that I had received Christ by faith as a child and accepted the word of God by faith, and that was it. From that point on, I did my very best to do or not do what the Bible proclaimed, through my own effort and not by faith. Finally I realized that I must claim, moment by moment, the word of God and His promises by faith. In other words the Bible says, "The just shall live by faith." That means taking a daily walk of faith. That means when I read a principle from the Bible with understanding, I must claim that principle for my life by faith. I must appropriate that principle to my life. This truth made me realize there is a saving grace and faith, a sustaining grace and faith, and a living grace and faith. Appropriation has to do with our everyday living in grace and faith.

An Example of Appropriation

The apostle Paul told the church in Philippi, "Be anxious for nothing, but in everything by prayer and supplication, with thanksgiving, let your requests be made known to God" (Phil. 4:6 NKJV). In other words Paul simply said, "Don't worry or be anxious."

Do you worry? If so, are you able to overcome that worry in your life? If your answer to that question is no, then the next question would be, "Why do you not have the faith to claim God's word from the Bible to overcome worry?" For this directive of overcoming worry to be a reality in your life, you must accept Paul's very simple statement at face value through faith. You must appropriate or, in other words, claim this Scripture as your own by faith. By appropriating this Scripture today, you can overcome any worry and anxiety you may be experiencing.

Paul followed up his thoughts about worry by stating the promise of God if we overcome our worry by faith. "And the peace of God, which passeth all understanding, shall keep your hearts and minds through Christ Jesus" (Phil. 4:7). This is God's promise to us as we appropriate His word concerning worry in our lives. We must first pray and give our situation over to Him; if we do so, He has promised that we will experience peace in our minds and hearts. The elimination of worry from our lives isn't going to happen by accident, and that's because the Bible makes it clear that we must appropriate and claim the Scripture through faith.

Assimilation

Now we turn our attention to the word *assimilation*. The word *appropriation* deals with our *claiming* the word of God and its promises, whereas *assimilation* deals with our *applying* the word of God to our lives and actually living out the word of God in all our relationships. In other words it's the process of our digesting and absorbing the word of God into our spiritual lives so the word doesn't lie dormant in our minds but actually transfers to our hearts and becomes active in our everyday lives. This is similar to our physically digesting and absorbing the food we eat.

In reality you become what you eat because you've assimilated and absorbed the food you ate. The same principle holds true for your spiritual well-being. You become what you assimilate, digest, and absorb into your spiritual life. When you appropriate or claim the fruit of the Spirit as listed in the word of God and subsequently assimilate that very word into your heart, your life will radiate the life of Jesus Christ as you live through the power of the Holy Spirit. You will radiate His love, joy, peace, patience, kindness, goodness, faithfulness, gentleness, and self-control.

Why will you radiate the fruit of the Spirit? Simply because you will have assimilated and digested what you ate in your spiritual diet. This will bring you to a place where you no longer have to live in conflict, confusion, or pain; rather you can experience the power and presence of God in your life. It's here that Christianity *does* work! It is with a broken heart that you will find the abundance of joy and peace in your life.

Power to Enable Our Growth

The second principle we will look at in dealing with the growth of our spiritual lives is the principle that energizes the process, and that's what I call the "power." This is a more difficult principle to understand and practice, and it's possibly more difficult to implement in our lives, as we often resist such a change. We will look at the power from two different angles.

Our Outer Man
The first angle we look at concerning the power that enables us to grow is what the apostle Paul called the "outer man." For God's power to be a reality in producing spiritual growth in our lives, we must follow the apostle Paul's train of thought when he dealt with the outer part of man in Romans 7 as well as 1 Corinthians 2–3.

We must start from the outside and move inward if there's going to be a transformation in our lives. The outer man represents our physical bodies or what we call our "flesh." The Greek word for "flesh" is *sarx*, which often relates to the physical body. Paul calls it the "carnal man" in 1 Corinthians 3:3. Many of our early church scholars saw the flesh as being all of our body parts, constituting a totality of man known as "the flesh," which is dominated by sin. In theological terms it is often called the "sin nature."

Augustine referred to the flesh as the outer self or the external part of man. He considered the body as the fleshly shell in which we live and which relates to the outer or physical world. This part of man deals with and relates to our culture and the moral values that enter our person through the five senses. When I think of the flesh, I do so in terms of our self-centeredness, our egos, our arrogance, or our being in total control of our lives. I think of the head-to-head, confrontational behavior in our relationships, which I described earlier in this book. The flesh is the conflict, fighting, and fussing we're far too familiar with in our relationships.

The Bible tells us not to yield our flesh, or outer man, unto sin. In Galatians 5:19–21, we see the manifestation or the works of the flesh, the outer person, described as sexual immorality, impurity and debauchery, idolatry and witchcraft, hatred, discord, jealousy, fits of rage, selfish ambition, dissensions, factions, envy, drunkenness, and orgies.

A Blow to the Outer Man

The best way to picture what needs to be done so that we may truly deal with the flesh and render it ineffective in our lives is to take a look at a grain of wheat as described in the Bible. "Verily, verily, I say unto you, except a corn of wheat fall into the ground and die, it abideth alone: but if it die, it bringeth forth much fruit" (John 12:24).

So first we're going to take a look at the hard outer shell of a grain of wheat, which represents our hard outer shell called our flesh. We want to learn from the Scriptures what God has to say about a grain of wheat's outer shell being softened. This softening allows that outer shell to be broken open so that what is on the inside of the grain can sprout and come forth to produce fruit.

The softening of the hard outer shell or flesh of our lives represents the brokenness in our lives. You will notice in our Scripture that God says we will abide alone until He is able to bring brokenness into our lives. The reason we so often experience loneliness is because we aren't willing to die to the self, to relinquish control of our lives to God, and to allow Him, through brokenness, to soften our outer shells. Anytime we relinquish control of our lives to God, it will deliver a blow to our egos. Then, and only then, will we live fruitful lives. You see, the hard outer shell of our lives hinders anyone from penetrating our lives or, on the other hand, for our lives to break forth and be invested in other people. Thus, as the Bible declares, we stand alone.

Wheat grain can be stored for thousands of years. Stories have been told of the ancient Egyptians placing grains of wheat in the pyramids in case the Pharaoh got hungry in the afterlife. Supposedly scientists have planted grains of wheat from those pyramids, and the wheat germinated. After the hard shell softened and was broken open, the innermost part of that grain of wheat, which had lain dormant for thousands of years, was turned loose and energized to bear fruit.

Whether the Egyptian stories are true, we do have from the heart of God, recorded in His word, the principle of a grain of wheat that will remain a single grain of wheat, standing alone, until it is planted. Once planted, it will die only to later produce a head of wheat with multiple grains. In other words that single grain is now capable of bearing fruit because it has died, or the outer shell has been broken.

Our Inner Man

The second angle we will look at is God's power to enable our growth in that part of us the apostle Paul called the "inner man." Paul addressed that part of us when he said, "For I delight in the law of God after the inward man" (Rom. 7:22). I would venture to say that everyone reading this book has a desire similar to that of the apostle to "delight in the law of God after the inward man." The problem is that we still struggle with another law that yanks and tugs at the inner man, as we see in verse 23: "But I see another law in my members, warring against the law of my mind, and bringing me into captivity to the law of sin which is in my members." In other words this struggle occurs in the outer man.

Because of the constant battle between the flesh and the Spirit, or between the outer man and the inner man, we find ourselves in that confused state discussed earlier in the book. Once the outer man is broken, however, we can live with yielded lives to the Holy Spirit. Once we've yielded, we find a law or principle that can override the law of the outer man or the flesh. Paul spoke of that principle to the church at Rome. "For the law of the Spirit of life in Christ Jesus hath made me free from the law of sin and death" (Rom. 8:2).

The law, as we see in this Scripture, is what we often call a principle. As I mentioned earlier, we can illustrate the law as a principle by noting how one law can override another law — for example by observing an airplane soaring in the skies. At that moment we see the law of aerodynamics overriding the law of gravity. The law of the Spirit of life in Christ overrides the law of sin and death. It is at this point that Christianity works!

The Makeup of the Inner Man

The inner man consists of the soul and spirit. It is the real you, the part that allows you to relate to other people and God. The soul consists of the mind, emotions, and will. It allows you to relate to yourself and to people. The spirit is that part of you that allows you to relate to God and to have a personal relationship with Him. It is our spirits that are dead in our trespasses and sins but are made alive when we receive Jesus Christ as our personal Savior. We call that "being born again." At that time the Holy Spirit enters our spirits to dwell in us. Now we have a principle, or a law, that overrides sin and death.

Since the Holy Spirit dwells in us, through the brokenness of the outer man, we can begin to experience true victory to live. People around us, in our various relationships, begin to see that victory in our lives. They see the work of the Holy Spirit sprouting, growing, and producing fruit in our lives. God's life now flows from us and overrides the works of the flesh in our lives. Before our brokenness the fruit of the Holy Spirit — love, joy, peace, patience, kindness, goodness, faithfulness, gentleness, and self-control — wasn't able to penetrate and break through our outer, hardened shell. Since the fruit of the Spirit couldn't break through, everyone around us saw only the works of our old, fleshly life instead of the wonderful works of Christ emerging from our lives.

The Peace of the Inner Man

You have God's life within you all the time, but until you die, you stand alone; in other words you're just one grain of wheat. Once you die, however, your inner life germinates and comes forth so that you can bring forth much fruit and become many grains. God provides the power for this transformation, which allows that transition from the outer man to the inner man through brokenness or a contrite heart. Now people will see not the conflict of your outer person but the peace of your inner person emerging in your daily life. This is the journey of transformation God has mapped out and is working out in your life.

Brokenness may come our way through many avenues. It may come through deteriorating health, the loss of our wealth, a shattered relationship, a deep depression, or an anxiety attack. Very possibly brokenness may come because of foolish choices we or others may have made in our relationships with them. It is also possible that God may bring painful experiences of brokenness about in our lives as a way of lovingly disciplining us. We will never shorten the time of the brokenness God allows into our lives, because He is in control of that time. However, we may lengthen the time of our brokenness if, through our lack of understanding or stubbornness, we refuse to yield our lives to Him and do not allow God to break our outer shells.

The Purpose of Our Growth

For I know the plans I have for you; 'declares the Lord,' plans for welfare not for calamity to give you a future and a hope.
—Jer. 29:11 NASB

We now have journeyed through the pages of this book. My desire is that you now have a greater appreciation for your life's journey than you did before you started reading this. My prayer is that you see the spiritual journey you are traveling on as an incredible journey, one that can become an even more incredible journey than you could ever image.

If you're traveling through the principles of this book, or at least beginning to implement them into your spiritual life, you're well on your way to making the eighteen-inch journey from your head to your heart. It will bring you to the purpose for which God has made you and give you a future and a hope. God's purpose is never for us to live a life of calamity but to find hope for the future.

The principles outlined in each chapter of this book will override all the negative behavior we experience in our families and church relationships, which I described and discussed in the first five chapters of this book.

Isn't it amazing that such a challenging journey, which often seems so complicated, is only an eighteen-inch journey? Wow, the journey is so short, and yet it takes us so long to make it. Yes, it is an eighteen-inch journey from the head to the heart. Though it may be the most difficult eighteen-inch journey you'll ever make, it will be the most life-changing eighteen inches you'll ever travel. As you continue your journey, keep in mind the following two verses that describe where life is lived. Proverbs 4:23 states, "Keep thy heart with all diligence: for out of it are the issues of life," and Proverbs 23:7a says, "For as he thinketh in his heart, so is he."

Every journey has a starting point, when you insert the key and start the engine, and a finishing point, when you apply the brakes and turn off the engine. We're now at the end of this journey we made together through the various heart conditions. Would you allow me to toss out a couple of thought-provoking, challenging questions?

The first question is this: "Have you actually begun the spiritual journey by placing your faith and trust in the finished work of Jesus Christ on the cross of Calvary?" The Scripture says, "For by grace are ye saved through faith, and that not of yourselves: it is the gift of God: Not of works, lest any man should boast" (Eph. 2:8-9). If you haven't yet received Christ, I encourage you to pray and ask Him to come into your life and forgive your sins.

On the other hand, if you are already a Christian and have analyzed each chapter of this book, which depicts a particular leg of the spiritual journey, did you by any chance find where you are in your spiritual life journey? Which chapter best describes your spiritual location — your heart condition — today? At which juncture did you locate your heart? Do any of the heart characteristics described in this book — a corrupt, confused, curious, consumed, changing, or clean heart — apply to you today? Or perhaps you're in the stage of experiencing the brokenness of your spiritual life, and you now have a contrite heart.

Remember the question I presented earlier in the book? "Does Christianity work today?" I would like to answer that question unequivocally. Yes, Christianity does work!

I know this. As complicated, confusing, painful, and dysfunctional as your Christian life may seem at the present time — along with how fragile all our relationships may be today — the Christian life is an incredible journey. It's one that can bring you love, joy, peace, patience, kindness, goodness, faith, self-control, and meekness — all of which will provide rest for your soul. It truly is an abundant life.

My encouragement to you is this: don't give up on the journey. Stay the course, for it is worth the effort to finish the course well. The eighteen-inch journey will transform you from a frustrated, head-to-head, indifferent person to a peaceful, heart-to-heart, sensitive person in every relationship you have.

Praise God for the spiritual life journey! He has a destination just for you. The Holy Spirit will be your driver and guide you through the holy potholes of Christianity. Leave the driving to Him, and enjoy your journey!

About the Author

Albert Schuessler's roots are planted deep in the soil of a south-central Kansas farm. His parents gave him the road map of life at a very early age, along with the biblical principles of establishing, developing, and maintaining a spiritual journey.

He worked in the business world until 1968, when he enrolled in a Baptist Bible college in Springfield, Missouri. After graduating from Bible college, he entered the pastorate and has been following that dream for forty-six years, including pastoring at Faith Bible Baptist Church in Valley Center, Kansas, for twenty-eight years prior to his retirement.

His family has been a vital part of his life's journey. He has been married to his wife, Shirley, for fifty-six years. They have three sons, ten grandchildren, and five great- grandchildren. He is currently on the staff of Glenville Church in Wichita, Kansas.

This book is about his journey and what he learned while negotiating the potholes of his Christian life. Within the pages of this book, he talks about finding the road map of his life, which he temporarily lost while on his spiritual journey.

Made in the USA
San Bernardino, CA
20 October 2014